Saladin

Saladin

The Sultan and His Times, 1138–1193

HANNES MÖHRING

Translated by
DAVID S. BACHRACH

Introduction by
PAUL M. COBB

The Johns Hopkins University Press
Baltimore

© 2005 Verlag C. H. Beck OHG, Munich
Originally published as *Saladin: Der Sultan und seine Zeit, 1138–1193.*
English translation and Introduction © 2008
The Johns Hopkins University Press
2 4 6 8 9 7 5 3 1

The Johns Hopkins University Press
2715 North Charles Street
Baltimore, Maryland 21218-4363
www.press.jhu.edu

The translation of this work was supported by a grant from the Goethe-
Institut that is funded by the German Ministry of Foreign Affairs.

Library of Congress Cataloging-in-Publication Data
Möhring, Hannes.
[Saladin, der Sultan und seine Zeit, 1138–1193. English]
Saladin, the Sultan and his times, 1138–1193 / Hannes Möhring;
translated by David S. Bachrach; introd. by Paul M. Cobb.
p. cm.
Includes index.
ISBN-13: 978-0-8018-8991-2 (hardcover : alk. paper)
ISBN-10: 0-8018-8991-x (hardcover : alk. paper)
ISBN-13: 978-0-8018-8992-9 (pbk. : alk. paper)
ISBN-10: 0-8018-8992-8 (pbk. : alk. paper)
1. Saladin, Sultan of Egypt and Syria, 1138–1193. 2. Crusades.
I. Bachrach, David Stewart, 1971– II. Title.
DS38.4.S213M65 2008
956′.014092—dc22
[B]
2008006795

A catalog record for this book is available from the British Library.

*Special discounts are available for bulk purchases of this book. For more
information, please contact Special Sales at 410-516-6936 or
specialsales@press.jhu.edu.*

CONTENTS

No other Muslim ruler is as well-known in Europe as Sultan Saladin. Although he inflicted heavy losses on the Crusader states, he enjoyed a very favorable impression in the West for centuries. He is described in European historiography as a chivalrous opponent and the model of the "noble heathen." Very early on, legend transformed him into a secret Christian. In the age of Enlightenment, he was seen as an exponent of the ideal of tolerance. By contrast, for many Muslims today, he is above all a champion of freedom.

There can be no doubt that Saladin is among the outstanding figures in world history. His rise to a position as the most important man in the Near East of the twelfth century began in Egypt. For this reason, he was compared by friend and foe alike with Joseph of Egypt, well-known from both the Old Testament and the Qur'an. He destroyed the Fatimid caliphate in Cairo and usurped Nur al-Din's inheritance in Syria. The propagation of the jihad against the Christians served to legitimate his rule. In 1187, he succeeded in capturing Jerusalem. He maintained this conquest during his struggle against the Third Crusade.

The Arabic and Latin sources for the history of Saladin and his opponents are very rich. Despite the panegyric texts and the propaganda, these sources provide an opportunity that is rare in the case of a personage of the Middle Ages, namely to write the biography of a ruler that offers a glimpse of his personality.

Research on the Crusades plays a peripheral role in German universities, particularly in contrast to Anglophone scholarship. Now, as in the past, there are very few medieval historians who can read Arabic sources and engage with Islamic history. As a result, research on the Crusades continues to neglect Muslim affairs.

As the first biography of Saladin in German, this brief study is intended to help address this lacuna. This work is based largely on my own research. I hope that this text not only will provide a background to the reader but also will clarify the connection between past events and the current issues of religious tolerance and the relationship between holy war and political pragmatism.

The World of Saladin

PAUL M. COBB

We begin at the end. Saladin, founder of the Ayyubid dynasty, sultan of medieval Egypt and Syria, famed Muslim opponent of Crusaders, died on 4 March 1193. Having lived a remarkable life, Saladin's penchant for the exceptional persisted even after death. This is best appreciated in Damascus, where he is buried. To approach his tomb, one ducks into a discreetly labeled precinct just behind the recently refurbished exterior courtyard of the Umayyad Mosque, itself one of the most stunning examples of medieval Islamic architecture and the city's most important religious building. Inside the precinct of Saladin's tomb, one is immediately struck by the quiet and the cool shade, a welcome respite from the blinding Syrian sun and chattering visitors to the Umayyad Mosque just outside. But the most noticeable aspect of Saladin's tomb is encountered when one steps into the mausoleum proper and observes his sarcophagus. Or, rather, his sarcophagi: for there are two of them.

A quick scan over the sarcophagi solves the puzzle. One, a humbly carved wooden box draped in green cloth, is enclosed in glass to protect it. This is Saladin's original, medieval resting-place. The other is an ornate, baroque confection of carved and inlaid white marble, similarly draped. The latter was placed in the tomb in 1903, part of restorations paid for by the German kaiser Wilhelm II, an aficionado of Crusades history and one of many European admirers of the sultan. Not far from the tomb, another monument makes claims on Saladin's legacy. Just outside the walls of the old city, beneath the beetling parapets of the citadel used by Saladin's descendants, stands a large modern bronze statue of Saladin on horseback, accompanied by Muslim soldiers, and bearing Crusader prisoners in chains. This little walking tour epitomizes the place of Saladin in his world, and ours: few medieval Muslim rulers have merited modern statues; even fewer have two sarcophagi. Commemorated at once by his medieval Muslim peers, by modern European Romantics, and by contemporary Syrian nationalists, even Saladin's memory stands out in a crowd.

The Geographical Setting

As Hannes Möhring explains in this lively biography, Saladin wasn't always the toast of Damascus or Berlin, and yet his name persists in historical memory even while (or perhaps because) so many factors were stacked up against it. Take geography. The Middle East is only part of the broader medieval Islamic world, which covered an area more than three times than that of medieval Christendom. At its greatest extent, the medieval Islamic world extended from the Atlantic coast of Morocco and Spain in the west to western China and the Java coast in the east, from sub-Saharan Africa in the south to the steppes of Russia in the north. Even considered as but a smaller piece of this vast Islamic world, the Middle East (or the Near East as it is sometimes called) is not a region given to unities, a reality that Saladin must have appreciated as he crossed from Iraq toward Egypt at the start of his career and then later from Egypt toward Iraq as he conquered these lands for himself.

The parts of the Middle East that formed the arena for most of the events of Saladin's life are enclosed by the sequence of towns, cities, and water sources known popularly as the Fertile Crescent. At its eastern edge lies the river system formed by the Tigris and the Euphrates, which plunge in roughly parallel courses from their sources in the mountains of eastern Turkey (or "Anatolia" as historians call it) toward their final debouchments into the Persian Gulf. Iraq, the "land between the rivers"—Mesopotamia— has long been defined by these two mighty sources of water, wealth, defense, and communication. Northern Iraq, called the Jazira, or peninsula, because it is almost surrounded by these two rivers, had as its capital the city of Mosul, a springboard for many Muslim armies headed toward Syria and Anatolia. The Jazira is rugged country: it starts as mountains in the north, giving way to scruffy hills and finally the gentle, ancient, and fertile flood plain which descends south toward Baghdad and the Persian

Gulf. Between Baghdad and Mosul, a number of small towns grew up along the river and the roads serving it. One of these was Tikrit, Saladin's hometown.

West of the Euphrates, the Syrian desert stretches south without interruption into the arid Arabian peninsula, home to the Muslim holy cities of Mecca and Medina, before rising into the cooler mountains of Yemen. Northward, the Syrian desert gives way to the fertile lands of northern Syria, delimited by the forested slopes of the Taurus Mountains, the natural barrier between geographical Syria and Anatolia, and the Fertile Crescent's northern edge. As it extends to the west, the desert becomes rocky steppe and finally farmland, dotted by villages, roads, towns, and cities. In most of geographical Syria, passage further west is blocked by mountains, among them the snow-capped Lebanon Mountains and the Jabal Ansariye, and so this part of Syria is a north-south world. Syria's major cities hang like a pendant from the borders of Anatolia to the Red Sea: Aleppo, Hama, Homs, and the principal city of the region between Egypt and Iraq, Damascus, a verdant and well-watered oasis city as old as any city could claim to be. Parallel to the cities and the mountains, a seam can be traced in which sit numerous bodies of water, such as the Orontes River in the north, Lake Tiberias, and the Dead Sea. South of Damascus, the Jordanian steppe intrudes into the settled zone and the mountains of the north become the stony hills of Palestine, bordered by the River Jordan and its deep valley, the Ghor, that leads to the port of Aqaba (or Ayla) and the Red Sea.

The steep mountains of the north and the deep Ghor valley of the south mean that passage west from Syria was rare, precious, and strategically important. For example, in the north, near the city of Homs, a gap in the mountains allowed easy passage west into Lebanon and to the cities, towns, and ports of the eastern Mediterranean coast, like Tripoli and Acre; it was, as a result, jealously guarded by fortresses. In the south, the bridge at Jacob's Ford was one of the few places where large groups could cross the Jordan valley. Only after crossing into Palestine could one proceed to the Sinai peninsula and thence into the western edge of the Fertile Crescent: Egypt, the Nile valley, and its capital Cairo. In Saladin's world, Cairo was the greatest of Arab cities, capital of the Fatimid dynasty and, eventually, of Saladin himself.

Islamic Civilization in the Age of Saladin

Given this great regional variety, the Islamic civilization of the world into which Saladin was born was by necessity flexible, a result of the core structures of Islam, in particular the *shari'a*, or Islamic law, and the economic, political, and cultural power of the various Islamic states that held sway over the centuries. Islamic civilization was some five hundred years old when Saladin was born, yet it was still adaptive and could, on one hand, change to fit local needs wherever Muslims predominated and yet, on the other, retain a recognizable pattern throughout. As such, it stood as a source of wonder and anxiety to other civilizations, even older ones such as those of medieval Christendom. To understand Saladin's world, it will serve us well to consider briefly the development of Islamic civilization prior to the age of the Crusades.

Islam itself has its origins many centuries before Saladin's day in the small towns and tribal politics of seventh-century Arabia. Muhammad, Islam's prophet, saw himself as a restorer of an old creed, not a founder of a new religion. Muhammad's principal concern was to warn humanity to return to the pure and unadulterated monotheism embodied in the patriarch Abraham's covenant with God, a covenant that other monotheists (Christians and Jews) had woefully let lapse. To guide Muhammad and his followers, God sent him revelations, later collected as Muslim scripture (the Qur'an). In preaching these revelations, the Prophet enjoined his followers throughout Arabia to repent and to embrace submission (in Arabic, *islam*) to God's merciful commands, lest they be judged accordingly at the end of time. It was a message that, in many of its specific teachings, upset existing social mores. Yet Islam also united Arabia's fractious tribes and provided a certain moral urgency that focused the energies of the earliest believers.

Within a decade after Muhammad's death, in 632, his followers had conquered and settled much of the same territory that would, centuries later, fall to Saladin. During the first waves of the great Arab Conquests, Muslim armies absorbed the ancient Persian empire and the eastern provinces of the Byzantine empire, including Palestine and the holy city of Jerusalem, and crafted them into an Islamic empire—thereby encouraging the slow conversion of Jews, Christians, and Zoroastrians to Islam.

This striking new political situation shook the worldview of many non-Muslim observers within and outside of the Middle East. The loss of the Holy Land was particularly badly felt among the Christians of Byzantium and western Europe, who did not fully understand that the land was just as holy to their Muslim rivals.

In the first centuries of Islam, the Islamic lands were unified in theory by the caliph (Ar. *khalifa*), who was held to be the sole ruler of the entire Muslim community, a successor for the Prophet, though not a prophet himself. In theory, most medieval Muslims acquiesced to the political realities of the day and generally recognized the three phases through which the line of caliphs passed. These were: the Rashidun or "Rightly-Guided" caliphs, whose era (632–661) represents something of a pious golden age for the community in which the Muslims were led by men who had known the Prophet personally; the Umayyad caliphs, who oversaw the furthest extension of the caliphate from the capital of Damascus (661–750); and the 'Abbasid caliphs, who ousted the Umayyads in 750 and became the very emblem of Sunni religious authority for most of the Middle Ages and the force behind much of Saladin's own activities. The 'Abbasid caliphs chose Iraq as their central province, founding Baghdad as their capital, where, with a brief interruption, they remained for centuries. The 'Abbasid caliphs ruled in Baghdad throughout Saladin's life and afterward, until the city was sacked in 1258 during the Mongol invasions of the Middle East. Saladin was a Sunni sultan who spent much of his time in Damascus, and so, for him, the memory of the pious Rashidun, the Syrian Umayyads, and the legitimizing 'Abbasids all had something to offer.

However, in practice many Muslims disputed the claims of certain individuals or lineages to hold the office of caliph. The most notable such case was the followers of the Prophet's cousin 'Ali, who felt that he and his descendants were the only legitimate successors to the Prophet. They ignored the line of caliphs recognized by the Sunni community and instead venerated 'Ali's kin as their religious leaders, or imams; this group came to be known as Shi'ites. Over time, Shi'ites would successfully develop their own unique ritual practices, holidays, and legal and theological responses to their followers' dilemmas, becoming and remaining even today the most viable Islamic alternative to Sunnism.

In the centuries before Saladin's time, in the formative era of Islamic history, there were two primary trajectories in the development of Islamic civilization. The expansion of the caliphate in early Islamic times had led to social and economic changes that sustained a new, mostly Arab, Muslim urban elite and new Islamic religious and cultural expressions that were embraced by any Muslim with cultural aspirations. This early Islamic cultural efflorescence formed the classic foundations of what would, in Saladin's time, be taken for granted as the very basics of Islamic civilization.

On one hand, Islamic civilization was a product of the caliphate's new elites and the caliphal court. This courtly context gave rise to distinctive developments in Islamic art and architecture, literature, philosophy, science, and to the intermingling of Iranian and Hellenistic models with Arabic literary traditions, all of which served to bind together the disparate ethnic and religious components of the ruling classes into one caliphal elite. Under the Umayyads, this hybridization process was clearly in play in the decorative and architectural motifs in religious buildings and palaces, as in the Dome of the Rock in Jerusalem. The 'Abbasids expanded on this process, glorifying Arabic poetry while patronizing the translation into Arabic of Iranian, Indian, and Hellenistic literary classics and mythical and scientific lore.

On the other hand, Islamic civilization was the basis for the religious and social values of the Muslim populace, especially in the cities. Here, religious scholars (Ar. *'ulama'*) and mystics decisively shaped these ideals in public circles of education. The goal for most medieval Muslims was to live a life that was pleasing to God, and the guidance to do so could best be found in Islamic law and its sources. These sources included the Qur'an and the exemplary practice (Ar. *sunna*, whence "Sunni" or mainstream Islam) of the Prophet. The *sunna* was best accessed in the traditions (Ar. *hadith*) of the Prophet and his companions, which were vetted, collected, and organized around a vast number of topics. This interest in Qur'anic context, the life of the Prophet and his companions, and the reliability of traditions fostered an unparalleled interest in exegesis, history, and biography. But not all Muslims used these sources of religious law the same way, and as disputes over questions of legal theory grew, different schools of Sunni Islamic law—all equally orthodox—crystallized around the approaches to law proposed by certain venerated masters (only four such schools survive today). Moreover, ambiguities in the text of the Qur'an, coupled with confrontations with other creeds, encouraged some Muslims to seek answers in theological debate (Ar. *kalam*), which tried to synthesize theological rationalism with the directives of divine revelation and law. Finally, for those Muslims who found the answers of jurists and theologians too sterile or academic, asceticism and mysticism (known conventionally as Sufism) provided a fertile environment for the meditative pursuit of gnosis and the obliteration of worldly distraction. Naturally, some pursuits, such as poetry, music, and history, found a ready audience in both court and city. By Saladin's time, Islamic high culture was increasingly a synthesis of all of these strands, Sunni and Shi'ite, ascetic and courtly, mystical and dogmatic, Arab and foreign.

In an odd way, the Islamic world owes some of its cultural success to the caliphate's failure. Long before Saladin's time, the 'Abbasid caliphate had begun to fragment, replaced by an array of regional successor-states, some loyal to Baghdad, some not. Many were founded using the cohorts of military slaves (Ar. *mamluks*) that had become common in late 'Abbasid times; some were of nomadic origin, or at least based a large proportion of their armies upon tribal levies. This proliferation of competitive courts resulted in an explosion of cultural production in which the most gifted and mobile thinkers were amply rewarded, whether they wrote in Arabic or the new literary language Persian.

This cultural profusion also coincided with what has been called "the Shi'ite century," a period that saw a sudden growth in Shi'ite political power and cultural expression across the Middle East. Since Shi'ite sectarian identity was so strongly connected to the issue of the succession of the imams, it was not long before some Shi'ites disagreed about particular candidates, resulting in dissenting lines of imams. One of these was the Isma'ili sect, beginning in the tenth century, which recognized a different branch of imams than that recognized by mainstream Shi'ites. To spread their message and to thwart the hated 'Abbasids, the Isma'ilis even founded their own rival caliphate, ruled by the Fatimid dynasty, which took power in Egypt in 969 and, by Saladin's day, was the most powerful Shi'ite state around. The Fatimid caliphate would also unwittingly serve as the catalyst for Saladin's rise to power. Moreover, in the generation before Saladin's birth,

Ismaʿilism itself experienced a schism, as some Ismaʿilis broke off from the main sect and recognized a new line of imams descended from a Fatimid prince name Nizar. These Nizari Ismaʿilis, finding themselves a minority unwelcome by both Sunnis and other Shiʿites, moved their communities to inaccessible locations in the mountains of Iran and Syria, where they sorely vexed their foes, including Saladin and the Crusaders, and became popularly known in the West as the "Assassins."

Eleventh-Century Changes

Even without these developments in Shiʿite politics, Saladin's world in the twelfth century was above all defined by radical changes during the eleventh. This was thanks to a new element of cultural and political change that arrived in the form of the massive Turkish migrations into the Middle East. As they proceeded across Iran and toward Iraq and Syria, the Turks created new states characterized by a thin veneer of foreign military elites who deftly used patronage of cultural and religious intermediaries to rule over their urban populations. This eleventh-century transformation, spearheaded by the Seljuk dynasty of sultans, was arguably the most significant cultural shift since the time of the Prophet, bringing with it Central Asian social mores, a new nomadic population, Persian high culture, and a robust interest in Sunni devotional piety. The Seljuks were keen Sunnis, and dependent rulers: it is no accident that it was under them that the madrasa, or college of legal studies, first spread, as places to foster the growth of Sunnism but also as mechanisms by which the sultans could build alliances with the religious elites of the cities. Thanks to these new schools, amongst the majority of Muslims the marriage of mystical Sufism and Sunni scripturalism was increasingly becoming the hallmark of mainstream personal piety. In such a setting, of course, philosophical and scientific inquiry also continued unabated. And at a popular level, this period also saw a renewed interest in asceticism and in devotions like fasting, praying, giving alms, visiting holy sites, and so on undertaken beyond the call of religious duty. These sat alongside jihad (struggle against Islam's enemies), which many Muslims employed in their battles against the crusading Franks who had invaded and settled parts of the Levant. These meritorious hardships thus dovetailed nicely with the needs of the Turks and the men who worked for them, newly Islamized warrior elites that valued physical and martial feats yet desperately sought Islamic authenticity.

While the struggle between the regional powers of the Fatimids and the Seljuks and other Sunni rulers (like Saladin himself) could at times heighten tensions between ordinary Sunnis and Shiʻites, Muslims from both groups tended to live comfortably alongside one another and alongside non-Muslim communities as well. This was largely because Islamic law accorded to Jews and Christians at least a protected social and political status called *dhimma* (and so they were called *dhimmis*). Bigotry was never absent, of course, but as long as Christians and Jews paid a certain tax and kept their place, as fellow monotheists and "Peoples of the Book," they could practice their religion freely and be valued as subjects of the Islamic empire, not to mention as colleagues or neighbors. For all their recalcitrance, even the Franks had settled in nicely in the social and religious landscape of the Middle East by the time Saladin was born. As for Sunnis and Shiʻites, centuries of coexistence had familiarized both camps with each other, and, while there was certainly tension, among normal folk such religious differences between Muslims tended not to matter much.

As complicated as the religious landscape of the medieval Middle East was, it was further embellished by the region's ethnic diversity. The people that Saladin encountered on a daily basis belonged to ethnic groups that would be recognized today as Arabs, Persians, Turks, Kurds, Armenians, Africans, and Europeans, to name only the largest groups. Saladin himself was a Kurd. Kurds were a largely nomadic, rough-and-ready ethnic group that had for centuries held fast to the mountains of northern Iraq, eastern Turkey, and Iran, only occasionally becoming involved in the confused politics of the lowlands after the fragmentation of the ʻAbbasid caliphate. But since the Turkish invasion of these same regions in the eleventh century, the Kurds had been on the move; and, with their renowned military skills in high demand, many Kurds found a welcome place among the warrior elites throughout the medieval Middle East.

The Turkish dynasty that held this all together in the generations before the birth of Saladin was the Seljuk dynasty, usually based in Iran. Their leaders had been granted the title "sultan" by the ʻAbbasid caliph in Baghdad because of the services they rendered to the caliph and to Sunnism in general. Except for the chief administrator or vizier (Ar. *wazir*) and his cohorts of scribes, the men who served the sultans by helping them govern their empire were all military men, known by various titles. Any man who had troops who followed him or had the requisite social standing was an "emir," a word usually used for Arab princes these days but which denoted a commander in Saladin's day. The Seljuks liked to give their own princes training in statecraft before they became sultans in their own right, and so the princes often served as governors of provinces of their family's domains. But often they were sent as mere children, and so a particularly trustworthy or skillful commander was sent with them. These men were called *atabeg*s. Atabegs were expected to serve their charges as commanders of their army, but also as tutors and companions. Not every atabeg merited the sultan's trust, and it was quite common in some provinces for atabegs to dominate their young charges and to rule in their place. In faraway places, like Mosul and Damascus, the possibility that independent-minded atabegs would break away completely was always present.

To help the Turks govern, emirs and atabegs had large armies of horsemen and infantry, usually of Turkish, Arab, or Kurdish origin, and often containing men who were mamluks, that is, men of slave or servile origin. Typically, such men were captured prisoners of war who were manumitted by their commanders and trained as their soldiers. Commanders and the soldiers under them were rewarded with cash stipends and assignments of lands (or the responsibility to collect taxes from lands) called *iqta*'s. Despite the great diversity in their use, *iqta*'s in Saladin's day resembled medieval European fiefs in many respects (but of course they differed from them, too). Well-rewarded emirs got a farm or a village or even whole provinces as an *iqta*'. Commanders and governors of a higher rank were usually rewarded with an appropriate title as well, which they bore throughout their careers. Such titles usually described the bearer in terms of their relationship to the state (Ar. *al-dawla*) or to religion (Ar. *al-din*), resulting in such titles as Sayf al-Dawla, "The Sword of the State," and Salah al-Din, "The Restorer of Religion," the Arabic title that gave rise to the name "Saladin" employed by Western historians.

In such a context, then, Saladin began his career as a relatively recognizable character type within the Seljuk provincial elite. His father, Ayyub, and his uncle, Shirkuh, were just another two Kurdish emirs who had entered the service of the atabeg Zengi of Mosul, himself an appointee of the Seljuk sultan and, ultimately, of the 'Abbasid caliph in Baghdad. The Seljuks were deeply concerned that much of Syria—to say nothing of Egypt itself—was controlled by the Shi'ite Fatimids. Moreover, the continued presence of Crusader polities ruled by Christian Franks in Syria was a grave embarrassment to Seljuk power and 'Abbasid legitimacy. Like all the other atabegs and emirs who had worked for the Seljuks before him, the atabeg Zengi's brief was to combat these two obstacles to Sunni unity. Unlike his predecessors, however, Zengi succeeded spectacularly, gaining firm control of Aleppo, a city then rife with pro-Shi'ite sympathies, and even taking back Edessa (in 1144), the first of the Crusader states to fall to the Muslims. When, in 1154, Zengi's son Nur al-Din finally added Damascus to these domains, he was merely fulfilling his father's goals; when he sent his emirs, Shirkuh and the young Saladin, to Egypt, he was both thwarting Frankish designs in the area and threatening to topple the Fatimids once and for all—one step closer to realizing the Seljuk dynasty's master plan of Sunni unification.

The Fatimids had long since realized that the end was near, and they could do little to actively resist Zengi's ambitions in Syria and Egypt, but the Crusader states were another story. After all, in the wake of the First Crusade, of 1099, the Franks had, as they saw it, liberated the holy city of Jerusalem and the tomb of Christ himself from centuries of iniquitous infidel rule. To defend their achievement, they carved out four new principalities in the region, at Jerusalem itself, as well as at Edessa, Antioch, and Tripoli. But Edessa had fallen to Zengi, and Nur al-Din's men had made it to Egypt first. True, there still remained, in Syria, numerous independent emirs who did not answer to Nur al-Din—the Shi'ite Assassins among them—but a prescient Frankish observer could see that time was not on their side. Eventually, the Zengids and the Crusaders must engage in a final struggle for Syria.

But everyone had forgotten about Saladin. In hindsight, Saladin's decision to march from Egypt in 1174 and claim Zengid Syria for himself at Nur al-Din's death has a ring of the liminal about it—as if a new era was beginning, a Middle Eastern Rubicon being crossed. But in many ways, Saladin's great accomplishments as a state builder owed much to the policies of Zengi and Nur al-Din, for the playing field that now confronted Saladin in Syria was one that had been largely configured by Zengid hands. Saladin had three primary obstacles before him. The remaining Zengid princes and their men sought to hold on to what was left of their patrimony in the region; local Muslim rulers sought to retain their independence, even if it meant choosing sides; and the rulers of the Crusader states tried furiously to stanch their own internal weaknesses and buy time before Saladin consolidated his control over Muslim-held regions and turned his attention on them. From the moment he crossed out of Egypt until his death in Damascus, Saladin would exhaust every diplomatic, political, and military option to overcome these obstacles and come as close as any Seljuk official ever did to unifying the fragmented world of medieval Islam.

Arabic Sources for the Age of Saladin

Saladin's world was also a highly literate world, a fact for which historians can rightly be thankful. Saladin's contemporaries have provided us with many written sources in Arabic with which to reconstruct the life and times of this sultan, and later generations of chroniclers and writers did not neglect this period either (to say nothing of the Latin chronicles of the Franks and sources written by other non-Muslims). The chronicle was the most basic genre of Arabic historical writing. Arabic chronicles were often universal histories—vast, unwieldy things, beginning with the creation of the world and proceeding year by year through the course of Islamic history down to the author's own time. For the period under consideration here, perhaps the most important chronicle is that of Ibn al-Athir (d. 1233), who lived in Mosul and, because of his family's long service to a rival dynasty, does not always put Saladin in the best light. One can expect a rather more flattering portrait in a chronicle written by Abu al-Fida (d. 1331), who was himself a member of the Ayyubid ruling house and so a descendant of Saladin. Abu al-Fida was lord of Hama in Syria, and his chronicle reflects its Syrian context. But Egyptocentric chronicles of the times can likewise be found, as in the work of Ibn Taghribirdi (d. 1470), who composed, as it were, a universal chronicle of Egypt.

Saladin holds a special place in Arabic historical writing, for he was the subject of biographical interest early on. This is not so very odd, since biography was also a central genre of Arabic writing. Indeed, some of the great biographical dictionaries of medieval Islam are filled with data that help historians reconstruct the context of Saladin's world, as in the great *Wafayat al-Aʿyan (Obituaries of the Notables)*, compiled by Ibn Khallikan (d. 1282). Still, very few Muslim rulers were, as Saladin was, the subject of discrete monographs devoted to their lives. One of these was written by Ibn Shaddad (d. 1235), who served as the judge over Saladin's army. The other was by ʿImad al-Din al-Isfahani (d. 1201), who was Saladin's personal secretary. Unfortunately, only part of ʿImad al-Din's biography survives, though he did compose another work devoted to the conquests of Saladin's later years which employs so flowery and purple a style that it continues to perplex historians.

There also exist a number of dynastic chronicles, a genre somewhere between chronicle and biography, that are devoted to the Ayyubid dynasty that Saladin founded. These include the work of Ibn Wasil (d. 1298), a Syrian who served the later Ayyubids as a scribe and diplomat. But of most value to studying Saladin's life and times is the *Kitab al-Rawdatayn (Book of Two Gardens)* of the Damascene Abu Shama (d. 1268), which forms a double dynastic chronicle embracing the rulers of the Zengid and Ayyubid houses—Saladin's predecessors and his descendants. On the level of contemporary witnesses, one might also mention the travel account of the Spanish pilgrim and wayfarer Ibn Jubayr (d. 1217), who cast his analytic eye about as he passed through Saladin's domains, and the heavily autobiographical meditation on Fate called the *Kitab al-Iʿtibar (Book of Contemplation)*, written by Saladin's courtier Usama ibn Munqidh (d. 1188) and dedicated to him.

As the reader may have noticed from this very limited sampling, literary sources, not documents, tend to dominate our picture of Saladin's period. Arabic papyri from Egypt of this period are plentiful, but they are only now being adequately edited and analyzed. There are, however, Arabic chancery documents that were selected and preserved as models of their genre—semidocuments, if you will. These appear with some frequency in the sources described above and in the collected official correspondence of al-Qadi al-Fadil (d. 1199), Saladin's chief of staff. Finally, European archives have something to offer for this period, and one of

Hannes Möhring's great contributions to our understanding of Saladin comes from his investigation of these documents.

Saladin's Legacy

A few Latin documents aside, Europe's appreciation of Saladin had to wait before the sultan acquired the status of the "noble heathen" in the West that Hannes Möhring traces at the end of this portrait. There were many obstacles to Saladin's reception in the West. For most Christian Europeans, the Middle East was frozen in time, and pilgrims returning from the Holy Land presented a picture of a place where biblical land-scapes and lifestyles were still believed to have currency, where Jerusalem was a museum city filled with the topographical bric-a-brac of the Old and New Testaments, where Muslims and five centuries of Islamic history had been largely edited out. At best, learned Europeans knew that the Middle East was inhabited by people they called Saracens and Turks, but their creed was considered to be heathen or pagan; Islam did not merit consid-eration as a proper religion. Islamic rulers were said to be cruel despots, whether an *amiralmuminimus* (Ar. *amir al-mu'minin*, caliph) or, like Sal-adin, a mere *soldanus* (Ar. *sultan*, sultan)—it was too confusing to sort it all out. These people, it was whispered, were steeped in sorcery, decadence, and sin.

There were, however, some times and places where Europeans might gain a better picture of Islam and Muslims. In Muslim Spain, or An-dalusia as it was called, the best-known such place, Muslims cohabited with Jews and Christians on the very frontiers of western Europe. The same could be said for Sicily, which had only recently been conquered from the Muslims in the course of the eleventh century. And the Middle East in the age of the Crusades was, all expectations to the contrary, an-other such place of cultural encounter. Many of the Latin writings associ-ated with the Crusades, though steeped in vitriol, nevertheless also dem-onstrate a sharper knowledge of the realities of the Islamic world by Westerners than ever before.

Thus, among the war stories and pilgrim accounts, tales of Saladin's allegedly chivalrous behavior during the Third Crusade trickled into Eu-rope. There his image grew into myth and has remained lodged in the

European imaginary ever since. In a way, the reality and myth of Saladin epitomize the Western consciousness of Islam and the Middle East as a whole, shaped by centuries of received information, misinformation, and fantasy. In it the Middle East is sometimes adored as a place of wonders, sometimes reviled as a land of infamy. In the short and insightful biography that follows, Hannes Möhring peels back the mythical image of Saladin and shows us how it has developed since Saladin was commemorated (the first time) in Damascus, leaving us contentedly alone with the historical reality: here was a Kurd who rose to power in a world dominated by Turks, a Sunni who used a Shi'ite caliphate to launch his rise to fame, a unifier of a world fragmented by religion, ethnicity, and even by the very landscape, a counter-crusader whose largest fan base has always resided in Christendom. By any measure available to his medieval peers, Saladin exceeded all expectations and lived his life, as the reader will come to see, against the grain of history.

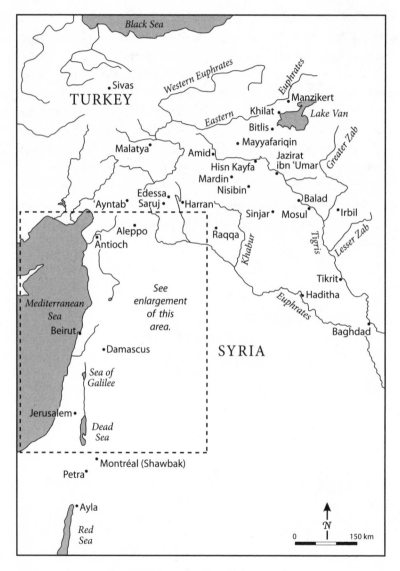

The Near East in the Time of the Crusades

Darbasak Tall Khalid •Mambij
Bagras •A'zaz •Buza'a
  Harim •Artah Aleppo
Antioch
    •Jisr al-Shughur Balis
Saône (Sahyun) •Burzayh Euphrates Qal'at Ja'bar
Latakia• Orontes •Ma'arrat al-Nu'man
Jabala•
    •Shayzar
Marqab• Masyaf •Hama
Tortosa•
Crac des Chevaliers• •Hims •Tadmur (Palmyra)
  Tripoli •'Arqa
Mediterranean Jubayl •Baalbek
Sea Beirut
  Sidon
Sarafand• •Marj 'Uyun
Tyre• •Banyas •Damascus
Toron (Tibnin)• *Hawran*
Acre• Saphet (Safad)
  Tiberias• •Ra's al-Ma'
Haifa• *Sea of Galilee*
Nazareth • •Belvoir •Salkhad
Caesarea • •Baysan (Kawkib) •Bostra
Arsuf• •Nablus
Jaffa•
  •Lydda Jordan
Jerusalem•
Ascalon• *Dead Sea*
Hebron• *N*

Karak• 0 150 km

Egypt and Palestine in the Time of the Crusades

Saladin

CHAPTER ONE

The Establishment of the Crusader States

The Expansion of the Caliphate

In a military campaign of unparalleled success, the adherents of the new religion of Islam advancing from the Arabian peninsula conquered North Africa and the Near East over the course of the seventh century. The Persian empire collapsed. However, its old rival, the Christian Byzantine empire, continued to survive despite the loss of Egypt, Palestine, and Syria. The Muslims became dangerous opponents even on the sea. During a second wave of expansion, they succeeded in driving the Byzantines step by step out of Sicily. The Muslims completed their conquest of Sicily in 902 and ruled there until losing the island to the Normans in 1091. From Sicily, the Muslims began to establish themselves in southern Italy. In 846, they plundered the district of Rome on the right bank of the Tiber. Later on, they laid waste the coasts of Sardinia and Corsica. In the far west of the empire, the Muslims had already begun driving northward over the Pyrenees by the early eighth century, but were defeated there. Nevertheless, over the long term, they occupied great parts of the Iberian peninsula and were not driven out until the end of the Middle Ages, following a centuries-long struggle against the Christian *Reconquista*.

In Christian eyes, the Islamic religion preached by Muhammad was the negative counterpart to Christianity. Muhammad is described in medieval European sources as a dangerous, immoral seducer. He is disparaged as a subversive, a false prophet, and the first-born son of Satan and the Antichrist. Without any close familiarity with Islam, Christians in Europe characterized it as a foul and corrupting doctrine that was both an error and a superstition. Its adherents were not designated as Muslims, but rather as Saracens, heathens, unbelievers, and the enemies of God, Christ, and belief, or as the sons of the devil and the supporters of the Antichrist, who was expected at the end of days. They were accused of idol worship and polytheism, although Islam is a rigidly monotheistic religion and rejects the Christian concept of the Trinity as polytheistic.

In contrast to the Christian image of Islam as a religion of ruthless violence, Muslims did not force Jews and Christians living under their rule to convert. They regarded them as adherents of distorted beliefs that had been superseded by the religion of Islam, but nevertheless as "possessors of the book" (Arabic, *ahl al-kitab*). When the Muslims captured Jerusalem in 638, they allowed the Christians to keep possession of the Church of the Holy Sepulcher, which had been built in the fourth century. Aside from the destruction of the Holy Sepulcher in 1009 by the Fatimid caliph al-Hakim (it was rebuilt several decades later thanks to skillful Byzantine diplomacy), the Muslims never contested Christian control over this holy site, despite the fact that Jesus played an important role in the Islamic religion as well. Like the Christians, the Muslims identified Jesus as the incarnation of God's spirit and word. They expected his return at the end of days and believed that he would kill the unbelievers with the breath of his mouth. In contrast to Christianity, however, in Islam Jesus is not seen as the son of God or as having risen from the dead. Rather, he is seen as having been carried off by God. After his return, he is expected to be buried in Medina alongside the Prophet Muhammad and the first two caliphs, Abu Bakr and 'Umar.

With the construction of the Dome of the Rock at the end of the seventh century, the Muslims established their own holy site in Jerusalem. Soon afterward, they built the Aqsa Mosque nearby. The name "Dome of the Rock" recalls sura 17.1 in the Qur'an, which records that Muhammad made a nighttime journey from "the holy place of worship" (Mecca) to the "distant place of worship" (Jerusalem). According to the legend, that same night the Prophet was taken into heaven from Jerusalem. In the course of this journey to heaven he is supposed to have left behind a footprint in the rock, still venerated by Muslims today, over which the Dome of the Rock was constructed.

Muhammad, who thought of himself as the prophet to the Arabs and apparently had no plans for the regions outside Arabia, died in 632. Acting as his representatives (Arabic singular, *khalifa*), the so-called "rightly guided" caliphs, Abu Bakr (d. 634), 'Umar (d. 644), 'Uthman (d. 656), and 'Ali (d. 661), took over the leadership of the Islamic community and the growing empire. As early as the caliphate of 'Umar, Islamic expansion had gone beyond the Arabian peninsula. Following the first four caliphs, who had attained their leadership roles through election, there were a dozen caliphs from the Umayyad clan. This clan had long been among the bitterest opponents of Muhammad, and their rule was fiercely contested by the supporters of 'Ali, who were designated as Shi'ites. In place of Medina, the Umayyad rulers chose to establish their capital in Damascus. When their rule was ended in the middle of the eighth century by the 'Abbasids, acting at that time in alliance with the Shi'ites, the center of gravity of the empire moved from Syria to Mesopotamia. It was here, at Baghdad, located on the Tigris River, that the 'Abbasid caliphs established the new capital and cultural center of the caliphate.

Fatimids and Seljuks

Although the 'Abbasid caliphate endured for several centuries, it began its decline as early as the first half of the ninth century. Step by step, the 'Abbasids lost power to the commanders of their Turkish guard, who eventually unified their control over financial and military affairs in the office of the emir of emirs. In addition, the outlying provinces of the caliphate began to achieve independence. It was in this context that the Fatimids, who conquered Egypt from their base in the Maghreb and established Cairo in 969, began to challenge the 'Abbasids for the leadership of the caliphate. The Fatimids were Isma'ili Shi'ites. They based their rule on the effort to establish an empire on behalf of the Mahdi, whom they expected at the end of the world, which they saw coming in the near future. The Mahdi was to ensure the spread of the true faith and of justice around the world. The Fatimids mobilized extensive propaganda efforts to bring about the defeat of the 'Abbasids. In addition to Egypt, they conquered Palestine and large portions of Syria. They also gained control of the holy cities of Mecca and Medina.

Independently of these events, the end of the tenth century saw the dramatic strengthening of Turkish influence in the Near East in a manner that was very dangerous for the 'Abbasids. Turkish peoples from Central Asia converted to Islam, moved westward, and adopted Iranian culture and techniques for organizing a state. Then, over the course of the eleventh century, they conquered Mesopotamia, Syria, and Anatolia. The Seljuk dynasty, whose leader was recognized as sultan (Ar. *sultan* = power or rule) by the 'Abbasid caliphs, provided a source of political cohesion for these conquests. It was in this context that the Seljuk sultan entered Baghdad in 1055 and seized power, legitimizing his rule as the defender of the faith against heretical enemies. The Seljuks distinguished themselves as the champions of the Sunna, that is, the Islamic orthodoxy, in the struggle against the Fatimids and the Byzantines. However, they were by no means the saviors of the 'Abbasid caliphate. Instead, they remained the constant rivals of the 'Abbasids. It was only when the power of the Seljuk central authority suffered a decline in the mid-twelfth century that 'Abbasid caliphs obtained, for the last time, a certain degree of freedom to act independently. Although their power was limited, in fact, to Mesopotamia, the 'Abbasid caliphs still maintained their claim that only they could grant legitimacy to the power enjoyed by other Muslim rulers.

In 1071, the Seljuks gained control of Jerusalem, which up to this point had been ruled by the Fatimids. The conquerors treated the Christians living there quite leniently and reserved their hate for the supporters of the Fatimids, whom they considered to be heretics. In addition, in 1071 the Seljuks inflicted a crushing defeat on the Byzantines at Manzikert in eastern Anatolia. From this time on, nomadic Turkish peoples infiltrated the Byzantine empire and moved throughout all of Anatolia. When the great Seljuk empire collapsed following the death of Sultan Malik Shah in 1092, Anatolia became part of the sultanate of the so-called Rum-Seljuks (Ar. *ar-Rum* = the Romans, i.e., the Byzantines), with its capital at Konya. The death of Malik Shah also led to a fragmentation of political power in Syria that lasted for more than a decade. At the end of the process, there was a system of Seljuk principalities in the Near East which was balanced on a knife's edge. It is this development that explains the constant change of political alliances in Syria during the first half of the twelfth century. The so-called Crusader states, newly established at the end of the eleventh century by the participants of the First Crusade, very soon were brought into this system of alliances.

The Origin of the First Crusade

In view of the difficult position faced by the Byzantines in Anatolia, Emperor Alexios I decided to send a request for help to Pope Urban II, despite the schism between the Latin and Greek churches dating back to 1054. When Urban held a council in Piacenza in March 1095, Byzantine emissaries were present. In the hope of recruiting mercenaries, they issued a request for military support. Because the emperor hoped for a particularly strong propaganda success, the envoys placed a special emphasis on requesting aid for Jerusalem.

On 18 November 1095, Pope Urban II convened a council at Clermont that was attended primarily by French bishops. This was the beginning of the First Crusade, which would be followed by several other crusades over the course of the next two centuries. The concept of crusade was a form of the idea of holy war, which at this time was already well-developed in Christian thought. In the narrower sense, a crusade was an armed pilgrimage undertaken as a military campaign by Western Christians. Intended to gain control over Christ's tomb in Jerusalem, it was organized and propagated by the pope. Participants were granted a remission of their sins. They also were required to take a vow to see this undertaking through to its conclusion. In a wider sense, leaving aside the question of pilgrimage and Jerusalem as a goal, the Crusade later could be understood as a war against the heathen or against the political opponents of the papacy.

It was only on the tenth day of the council, which was largely concerned with other matters, that Pope Urban gave a major sermon on the question of the Crusade. The crowds of listeners were so large that the sermon had to be held outside the city in an open field. The pope painted a vivid picture of the ostensible threat faced by Eastern Christians. He declared that the struggle against the Seljuks was the task of the knightly class, whose activities were being circumscribed by the Peace of God. This speech was extraordinarily effective. Filled with enthusiasm, many men, including some who had learned of Urban's intentions some time before, took an oath to undertake the struggle against the Muslims in the East. They cut their clothing into crosses and affixed these to their shoulders following the words of Matthew 10.38: "he who does not take up the cross and follow me, is not worthy of me." The decision by the council was that only those who went out of piety to free the city of God were promised a remission of the earthly penances imposed by the church. However, this meant much more, since, according to contemporary theological teaching, the decision to take part in the Crusade could only be made by a man who had already received from God a remission of his sins.

Urban II connected his summons to the centuries-old Christian tradition of pilgrimages to Jerusalem. The stream of European pilgrims to Jerusalem did not end after the conquest of Palestine by Muslim Arabs. A trade in relics kept alive the interest in the holy sites located there. Even more important, however, was the development of the penitential pilgrimage, which was imposed by the church as a penance for serious transgressions. These pilgrimages could take penitents to Rome, Santiago, or Jerusalem. The Crusader differed from the pilgrim only in that he bore arms, because he, too, carried the staff and pouch, the long-standing symbols of a pilgrimage. Characteristically, among other terms, the sources denoted the Crusade as a *peregrinatio*, that is as a pilgrimage. The term "crusade" itself first appeared in the mid-thirteenth century, as is demonstrated by the French word *croiserie*.

Despite the importance of the concept of pilgrimage and the idea of holy war, the motivation for such strong participation by the knightly class in the First Crusade cannot be attributed solely to the religious feeling, collective psychology, or the knightly ethos. Economic and social factors also played a role, as did the desire for adventure and hunger for booty. The East offered the enticing possibility of making one's fortune and of achieving a loftier position than one had in the homeland.

Excitement about the Crusade did not remain limited to Clermont and to France in 1095 and 1096. The bishops took steps to spread the pope's words to the people through the use of preachers. However, they were unable to prevent the undertaking from slipping partially out of their control. In early 1096, large and disorganized groups of people set out. Most of these people died on the journey in the Balkans or in modern-day Turkey. This "crusade" attained a sad sort of notoriety largely for the mass murder perpetrated by the participants against the Jews in numerous German cities they passed by on the course of their journey. These massacres were, by no means, the fault of just one man, such as the infamous Count Emicho of Flonheim. A major contributing factor, in addition to pure greed, was the idea of taking vengeance on the Jews for the death of Christ, or of forcing them to convert to Christianity.

Organized armies of knights from France and Norman southern Italy joined together at Constantinople, having set out several months later than the groups noted above. The Byzantines saw these armies more as a threat than as the assistance they had sought, and breathed a sigh of relief as these Crusaders departed imperial territory early in 1097 in the direction of Syria and Palestine. The idea of holy war remained a foreign concept to the Byzantines. In contrast to the West, the Byzantines did not believe that it was possible to achieve one's own salvation by shedding the blood of another.

The Crusaders in the Holy Land

Having arrived in northern Syria, the Crusade was in danger of collapsing before the walls of Antioch. The Crusaders were able to capture the city, in June 1098, only after an eight-month siege. Three weeks later they took the citadel. However, they did not return Antioch to the Byzantine emperor as they and the Byzantines had agreed at Constantinople. Rather, the Norman leader Bohemond established his own principality there. This came after Baldwin of Boulogne, later the first king of Jerusalem, had established himself as the ruler of Edessa, in March 1098. In 1099, the Crusaders resumed their march toward Jerusalem, which a short time before had fallen back into the hands of the Fatimids. In proposing an alliance with the Crusaders under the condition that they not enter Palestine, the Fatimids demonstrated their failure to appreciate the nature of the Crusade. The Crusaders occupied Bethlehem on 6 June. However, their first assault on Jerusalem, on 13 June, failed. It was not until a month later, on 15 July 1099, that Godfrey of Bouillon and his Lotharingians stormed the city walls and opened the gates of the city to their comrades in arms, thus capturing the holy city. After three years, they had finally achieved their goal, but their will to carry on was by no means exhausted. Some of the Crusaders decided to remain in the East rather than return home. It was up to them to stabilize what they had won and hold it over the long term. Following the establishment of the county of Edessa, the principality of Antioch, and the kingdom of Jerusalem, the last of the so-called Crusader states, the county of Tripoli, was created by the capture on 21 July 1109 of the port city of Tripoli after a year-long siege. However, it took several more decades before the Crusaders gained control over the entire coast of the eastern Mediterranean with the capture of Tyre in 1124 and Ascalon in 1153.

The capture of Jerusalem led to a dreadful bloodbath. As the Crusaders forced their way into the city, many Muslims sought refuge in the Aqsa Mosque in the Temple district, which was called al-Haram al-Sharif in Arabic. Having arrived there, they provided a large ransom and placed themselves in the custody of the Norman Tancred. His men had already seized control of the Dome of the Rock and plundered it. Tancred's banner, which was planted at the Aqsa Mosque, did not provide them with the protection they had foreseen. With the exception of the city governor, his troops, and some Jews, who were able to defend the citadel of the Tower of David and then secure free passage to Ascalon, the Crusaders killed most of the inhabitants of Jerusalem in an orgy of blood. This likely included Eastern Christians who were killed as a result of the confusion. The next day, some of the conquerors even broke into the Aqsa Mosque and killed all of the Muslims who had sought safety there. Things were no better for the Jews who, apparently, had defended the walls of Jerusalem alongside the Muslims. Most of them fled to their places of prayer, the synagogues, which were mercilessly burned along with the people who had taken refuge there. Others were sold as slaves, but most were redeemed through the donations of their coreligionists from elsewhere. Jews and Muslims were forbidden to live in Jerusalem. In their place, King Baldwin I settled Melkite Christians from the region of Transjordan in the city. However, he was not able to make up the severe losses in population.

It may seem astonishing that the Muslim holy sites were not destroyed. Godfrey of Bouillon converted the Dome of the Rock, which the Crusaders identified as the Temple of the Lord (*templum domini*), into a foundation for secular canons. Later this foundation was converted into a house of regular canons. The Aqsa Mosque, which from this point on was called either the palace or temple of Solomon (*palatium* or *templum Salomonis*), was chosen by Godfrey to serve as his own residence. In 1119, King Baldwin II granted a portion of the mosque to the newly established Order of the Knights of the Temple to serve as their headquarters. Ten years later, the entire mosque was given to them. Despite several stages of reconstruction, the prayer niche (Ar. *mihrab*) built by Caliph 'Umar remained in place and visible. This was also true of the Arabic inscription on the ceiling that even contained a citation from the Qur'an.

The oldest altar in the *templum domini* allegedly was established in 1101. However, it was not until 1141 that the Dome of the Rock was consecrated as the Church of St. Mary. Although the rock, which was holy to Muslims, was covered with marble flooring over which a choir and the high altar were built, the Arabic Qur'anic inscriptions remained untouched. The Crusaders were content to add Latin inscriptions that did not cover the Arabic text. These circumstances are even more astounding considering that the oldest Arabic inscriptions in the *templum domini* deny Jesus' status as the son of God and the Trinity. They also praise Muhammad as God's envoy and intermediary for Muslims at the final judgment. Although the Crusaders recognized that these were Arabic inscriptions, they apparently did not know their content. They did not know that the Dome of the Rock had been built by Muslims. Above all, they connected it with the episodes in the New Testament that took place at the Temple. Thus, for example, the footprint that was venerated by the Muslims as belonging to Muhammad, was transformed into Jesus' footprint. Of particular importance was the story, known to both Muslims and Christians, of the three-year-old Mary being accepted among the Temple virgins. As they did with other Muslim traditions that were connected with the Temple district, the Crusaders apparently adopted the Muslim identification of this place as being connected to the legend of Mary the Temple virgin.

Under Christian rule, Muslims were forbidden to live in Jerusalem. However, they were permitted to visit the Dome of the Rock and the former Aqsa Mosque as pilgrims. Probably, in the other regions of the kingdom of Jerusalem, Muslims were also permitted to visit the holy sites they venerated, such as the tombs of Abraham, Isaac, Jacob, and Joseph in Hebron. In some periods, these pilgrimages provided a rather lucrative business for Christians.

The Position of the Muslims under Christian Rule

Many Muslims refused to accept the new rulers and migrated to Syria or Egypt. They did not leave simply because they had been forced to do so by the Christians, or because of massacres perpetrated by the Christians at Jerusalem and Antioch (1098), Haifa (1100), Caesarea (1101), Tortosa (1102), Beirut (1110), as well as the massacres that were carried out in breach of agreements at Maʿarrat al-Nuʿman (1098), Acre (1104), and Tripoli (1109). In general, the Muslims held the view that Muhammad's example in leaving the then-heathen city of Mecca required them to leave their homelands rather than live under Christian rule. They felt that living under Christian rule would make it impossible for Muslims to remain faithful to their religious obligations and would place them in danger of becoming apostates.

In the case of the cities of Baisan, Jaffa, Ramla, Tiberias (all captured in 1099), Artah (1105), as well as Balis and Manbij (both in 1110), we know that the Muslim populations fled in face of the Crusader advance. In those cities that surrendered on condition that the population would be free to depart, as at Arsuf (1101), Acre (1104), Tyre (1124), and Ascalon (1153), all of the Muslims who were able to do so appear to have left. In such cities that were taken by storm, the population was driven out, as at Hebron (1099), or killed or enslaved, as at Maʿarrat al-Nuʿman (1098), Haifa (1100), Caesarea (1101), and Tortosa (1102), if they were not able to escape at the last moment.

In the period following the massacres in the towns captured up to 1110, there were no further persecutions of Muslims or Jews in the Crusader states, nor were there any efforts at forcible conversion. We know with respect to the conquest of Haifa in 1100, which ended in a massacre, that the Crusaders attempted to force the Muslims to accept one of two options: either convert to Christianity and thereby keep all of their properties and rights, or remain Muslims and lose all of their properties. In the latter case, the Muslims were supposed to have had the choice of either departing or subjecting themselves to Christian rule. It remains unclear whether the Crusaders offered similar alternatives to the Muslim inhabitants of other cities in the period before the capture of Sidon in 1110.

It remains a question whether some portion of the departed population returned to the cities noted above or if free Muslims lived there alongside Muslim slaves. Evidence regarding these questions is available only for Tyre. Nevertheless, when Jubail and Beirut were recaptured by Saladin in 1187, the majority of the population in both places is reported to have been Muslim, presumably not all slaves. This was true despite the fact that the Crusaders plundered the Muslims of Jubail in 1104, after having made a security agreement with them, and massacred the Muslim population of Beirut in 1110. It is very likely that there were mosques in those cities in which free Muslims lived. However, in contrast to the situation in Norman Sicily but analogous to the restrictions imposed on Christians living under Muslim rule, the call of the muezzin may well have been forbidden. Admittedly, there is evidence for mosques only in Nablus and Tyre. In these two cities, at least, there were probably also Shi'ites, whose numbers perhaps surpassed those of the Sunni Muslims living there.

In the rural districts of the kingdom of Jerusalem, it appears that the Muslims represented a majority of the population. Among these Muslims, slaves likely accounted for a higher percentage of the population than in urban areas. This is in contrast to the principality of Antioch and the county of Edessa, where Christians made up a majority of the population. Probably, many villages were either completely Muslim or completely Christian. As a result of this separation, the Muslims probably were not disturbed in the practice of their religion.

There was substantial unrest in the region southwest of Nablus in the middle of the twelfth century. In one of the villages there lived a legal scholar whose Friday sermons (Ar. *khutba*) attracted many Muslims from nearby. This fact, and perhaps the contents of his speech, raised the concerns of the local lord, who earlier had imposed higher than normal head taxes on the Muslims and had also introduced the cutting off of the feet as a punishment. He believed that the farmers were unnecessarily kept from their labor by their attendance at the Friday sermons, and therefore decided to kill the scholar. The latter, however, managed to escape to Damascus. Despite the resistance of their Muslim neighbors, his family was also able to flee. Other people who had heard him preach secretly left their homeland, too. In total, 155 people known by name fled from nine separate villages. In the other regions of the kingdom of Jerusalem, Muslim farmers also appear to have led hard lives. However, according to the report of Ibn Jubayr, an Andalusi pilgrim to Mecca who was an eyewitness to the events he describes, the taxes imposed on the Muslims in the kingdom of Jerusalem were not as high as those of their coreligionists living under Muslim rule.

Given this, it is hardly surprising that the sources very seldom mention revolts by Muslims in the Crusader states. Undoubtedly, not all Muslims found living under Christian rule to be an intolerable burden. This is demonstrated by their mourning at the death of King Baldwin III in 1163. It is reported that they came down from the mountains in order to pay their last respects as his body was carried from Beirut to Jerusalem. Unfortunately, it remains unclear what the king had done to earn this respect.

Some Muslims living in the Crusader states even converted to Christianity voluntarily. It was not only Christians who made pilgrimages to the cathedral at Tortosa, which was reportedly the oldest church dedicated to the Virgin Mary. Such Muslims, who believed in miracles, also traveled there in order to have their sons baptized so that they would live long lives or would regain their health. Above all, however, Muslim slaves desired to convert because they hoped in this manner to gain their freedom. It was this hope rather than any sort of religious feeling that motivated them. Most Christian lords, however, resisted the desire of their slaves to be baptized. Therefore, it was prescribed by law that a baptized slave who fled from his master and settled somewhere else in the kingdom was not to obtain his freedom.

CHAPTER TWO

Crusade and Jihad

The Crusades in Muslim Eyes

For Islamic history, the most important political consequence of the Crusades was the long-term union of Egypt and Syria under a single ruler. However, the danger posed by the Crusades to Muslim-ruled lands should not be overestimated. Following the capture of Jerusalem and all of the coastal cities of the Levant, the Crusades did threaten Damascus and even Egypt on several occasions; but Baghdad, the capital city of the caliphate, and the two holy cities of Mecca and Medina were never in danger.

There also can be no doubt that the reconquest of Jerusalem by Sultan Saladin in 1187 meant far more to the great majority of Christians in Europe than it did to the Muslims living in the East. Although Jerusalem was seen by Muslims as a holy city and as the site of the Last Judgment, in their eyes it was considerably less important than Mecca and Medina. The Muslims' dedication to the jihad against the Crusaders cannot be compared with the latter's efforts in Christian holy war, despite the promise of reward in the next life and the vigorous propaganda efforts by Saladin.

The period of the Crusades was a golden age for historiography in Syria and Egypt. However, the struggle against the Crusaders was far from the central theme of these works, just as events in Europe were of very little interest, in general, to Muslims. They originally believed that the First Crusade was an undertaking by the Byzantines, against whom they had fought for centuries. Admittedly, by 1105 comparisons were already being made on the Muslim side between the Christian crusade and the Islamic jihad. Nevertheless, it was not until decades later that the true nature of the Crusades—a concept that was also foreign to the Byzantines —became clear to the Muslims, namely that it was a pilgrimage combined with a military campaign to liberate Jerusalem in which the pope as initiator played a central role. Obviously, the most important factor in disseminating this information was Saladin's propaganda during the Third Crusade. All things considered, however, the Muslims very early on did see a connection among the Spanish *Reconquista*, the Norman reconquest of Sicily, and the Crusades in the East.

The conquest of Jerusalem and the foundation of the Crusader states did not immediately lead to a determined resistance by the neighboring rulers on the Muslim side. Nor was there a large-scale and spontaneous outbreak of holy war, despite the long tradition of volunteer warriors for the faith. Even in the later decades under Saladin, Muslim volunteers remained a small minority in the jihad against the Crusaders. The declining power of the Isma'ili-Shi'ite caliphate of the Fatimids in Egypt contributed considerably to the success of the First Crusade. More important was the splintering of the Seljuk empire and the ongoing rivalry among the Turkish rulers in the major Syrian cities. Moreover, there was virtually no noteworthy military cooperation between the Egyptians and the Turks in the struggle against the Crusaders, denoted as "Franks" (Ar. Ifranj or Faranj).

Rather, the Egyptians and Turks were willing to make agreements with the Franks. The Turkish rulers of Syria's cities succeeded in bringing the foreigners into their diplomatic game and in making use of them for their own interests as a new power factor. The existence of the Crusader states was of significantly less concern to them than the danger posed by an increase in the power of the Fatimid caliphate in Egypt or the Seljuk sultans in Mesopotamia. The Franks were receptive to these offers of alliance and were just as willing as the Muslims to make arrangements with enemies of their faith against their own coreligionists. It was characteristic of this Syrian state system that, in order to maintain the political balance of power, Frankish and Turkish ruling elites stood together to resist threats by non-Syrian powers, even against the resistance of the (non-Frankish and non-Turkish) populations they ruled. Thus, in 1115, a grand coalition of the Crusader states with Aleppo, Damascus, and Mardin shattered the efforts of the Seljuk sultan to reconquer Syria. However, alliances of this type in no way hindered the efforts of the erstwhile allies to expand at each other's expense once the external danger had dissipated.

The Instrumentalization of the Concept of Jihad

The First Crusade did not provoke a comparable reaction, that is, a campaign of holy war, among the Muslims. In contrast to the Seljuk sultan, neither the 'Abbasid caliph in Baghdad nor his Fatimid rival in Cairo developed even a rhetorical strategy for the struggle against the Franks. The Turkish armies that were sent out on jihad to Syria from northern Mesopotamia beginning in 1106 cannot be seen as signaling a counter-crusade by a unified Muslim world. The propagation of the jihad concept and the call for the unification of all Muslims in the struggle against the Franks simply provided the rulers in northern Mesopotamia, as well as those in northern Syria, with a tool to legitimize their feuds among themselves. Admittedly, aside from the campaign in 1115, the strikes launched out of Mesopotamia against Syria were organized by the atabegs of Mosul rather than the Seljuk sultan, and they were presented as support for the Syrian Muslims against the Franks, but these campaigns were not the result of Muslim ideas of unity. Rather, they are explained by conflicts within Iraq and the expansionist policies of the Seljuk sultan and the rulers of Mosul. They were not intended primarily to bring Frankish rule to an end. Nevertheless, the resonance of Syrian requests for aid at the caliphal court and in the mosques of Baghdad played a major role in ensuring that these campaigns took place.

The turning point in the relationship between the Crusader states and their Muslim neighbors in Syria was not brought about by the power of the idea of jihad but rather by the unification of Mosul and Aleppo under the rule of the Turk 'Imad al-Din Zengi. Aleppo opened its doors to him in 1128, the year after the Seljuk sultan had entrusted him with the government in Mosul. The result was a transregional power center. From this point on, Aleppo was no longer a possible ally for the remaining, independence-minded Syrian powers.

Zengi is normally seen as a protagonist of the jihad and an early champion of the union of the independent Islamic states for the struggle against the Franks. In fact, however, the threat posed to the Muslims by the Franks simply provided Zengi with an argument to support his demand that the Seljuk sultan give him the nominal overlordship of Syria to go along with having been named atabeg of Mosul. As his predecessors in Mosul and the Seljuk sultanate had done, Zengi used the concept of jihad as a tool to expand his own power. It is not until 1137 that we notice an official jihad propaganda effort during Zengi's reign or a particular interest in the Crusader states. Only after 1146, during the reign of his son and successor, Nur al-Din, did the idea of driving the Franks from Jerusalem and the coast region become a propaganda theme.

When Zengi tried unsuccessfully to conquer Damascus, in 1135, the Muslim and Christian powers in Syria realized that he was a serious danger. However, the military campaigns by the Byzantines into northern Syria in 1137 and 1138, which included an assault on Aleppo (1138), induced Zengi to continue in the Syrian tradition of maintaining a balance of power by seeking an agreement with Damascus and the Crusader states. The Byzantine campaign led to closer ties among all of the Syrian powers. It is in this context that Zengi married the mother of the prince of Damascus in 1138 and received Hims as a dowry.

After the murder of Shihab al-Din Mahmud of Damascus on 23 June 1139, Zengi renewed hostilities against this city. However, as was the case in 1135, the resistance there was too great, so he decided to attack the city of Baalbek, which apparently fell to him on 10 October. The garrison of the citadel offered to surrender several days later if he would guarantee their safety (Ar. *aman*). Zengi promised to do so, but he did not keep his word. He crucified all of the members of the garrison who did not succeed in fleeing.

Damascus and Jerusalem

It soon became clear that this breach of agreement was a serious error, because it wrecked any hope of gaining control of Damascus without a fight. The Damascenes feared that they would suffer a similar fate. The military resistance by Damascus against Zengi during the fall and winter of 1139 was supported by the entire population. In keeping with the traditions of Syrian alliance politics, early 1140 brought an agreement with

King Fulk of Jerusalem, who promised to provide military aid to Damascus. In return, he was to receive a substantial monetary subsidy to support his military efforts and the city of Banyas, which had been held by Zengi since 1137 and thus had to be liberated. The decisive reason for an alliance was the recognition that neither Damascus nor the Crusader states would be able to sustain themselves if Zengi's power spread further to the south.

The allies began their siege of Banyas in May 1140, and the city capitulated in the middle of June, following a guarantee to the defenders that they could depart safely and a promise of a Damascene military fief (Ar. *iqta'*) to the commander of the garrison. The conquerors promised that those who wished to remain in place would live under favorable terms. Following another failed attack on Damascus, Zengi retreated north. The alliance directed against Zengi led to a long period of peace between Jerusalem and Damascus, during which Mu'in al-Din Unur, the regent of Damascus, visited the holy sites in Jerusalem.

Zengi never returned to Syria. However, the period 1138–1144 saw ongoing hostilities between the principality of Antioch and the county of Edessa on one side and and groups of Turkmen and Zengi's governor in Aleppo on the other. When Joscelin II left his capital of Edessa in 1144 to bring military assistance to the Artuqid ruler of Hisn Kayfa, Zengi was able to capture the largely unprotected Edessa in December of that year. This brought the first major city of the Crusader states into Muslim hands. Over the course of the next two years, the Franks lost all of their territories east of the Euphrates River.

Zengi was celebrated as a hero of Islam and was given the titles "Zayn al-Islam," "Nasir Amir al-Mu'minin," and "Al-Malik al-Mansur" by the 'Abbasid caliph in Baghdad, meaning Jewel of Islam, Helper of the Commander of the Faithful (i.e., the caliph), and the (Divinely Aided) Conquering King. Zengi did not live to see the Second Crusade, which was organized in Europe in response to his capture of Edessa. In the middle of September 1146, he was murdered by a Frankish slave while he lay in a drunken stupor. As was true of so many other Muslim rulers, Zengi did not obey the Islamic ban on alcohol.

The death of Zengi, whose empire was divided between his sons Sayf al-Din Ghazi in Mosul and Nur al-Din Mahmud in Aleppo, quickly brought a change in the relationship between Damascus and Jerusalem. Unur, the regent of Damascus, forced Zengi's governor at Baalbek to give up control of the city and made truces and security agreements with Zengi's erstwhile officials at Hims and Hamah. Then he delivered Zengi's murderer, who had fled to Damascus, to Nur al-Din and began negotiations with the latter. These ultimately led to the marriage of Unur's daughter 'Ismat al-Din Khatun to Nur al-Din. In addition, Unur succeeded in having his rule recognized by the two caliphs, in Baghdad and in Cairo. Thus, the independence of Damascus was established on a more secure footing.

In contrast, the relationship between Damascus and Jerusalem went in the other direction when, in spring of 1147, the new Damascene governor of Bostra and Salkhad traveled to Jerusalem. The discussions that took place led the Franks to terminate their alliance with Damascus when the prevailing agreement expired. Unur and his son-in-law Nur al-Din were able to turn back the subsequent invasion by an army from Jerusalem into the region of the Transjordan. This failed campaign ultimately led to the reconquest of Bostra and Salkhad by the Damascenes. Up to this point, Unur had apparently hoped to maintain the peace between Damascus and Jerusalem in order to avoid having to ask Nur al-Din for aid, which would permit him to become involved in the affairs of southern Syria.

The appearance in the Holy Land by the participants in the Second Crusade worsened even further the relationship between Jerusalem and Damascus, since the Crusaders did not attempt to reconquer Edessa but rather undertook a campaign against Damascus in the height of summer in 1148. After fierce resistance by the Damascenes and the appearance at Hims of a relief army from Mosul and Aleppo—led by Zengi's sons Sayf al-Din and Nur al-Din, whom Unur very unwillingly had summoned to his aid—the siege of Damascus was broken off. The Second Crusade ended in failure.

By 1149, Damascus and Jerusalem, at Frankish request, concluded a two-year truce. Following the end of the Second Crusade, Unur returned to policies that he had pursued since Zengi's death. He did so despite the fact that contemporary poets praised the struggle against the Franks in 1147 and 1148 as jihad against the unbelievers and that religious emotions had reached a fever pitch during the siege of Damascus. Unur's decision was a response to the way Nur al-Din used his victory at Inab against Antioch at the end of June, achieved with Damascene military aid. Nur al-

Din managed to use this victory as well as his subsequent conquests to become the ruler over almost all of northern Syria. Following the death of his brother Sayf al-Din that autumn, Nur al-Din expanded his power in the subsequent dynastic conflict south to Hims and east to the region around the Euphrates tributary of Khabur. He also gained control of Zengi's former treasury at Sinjar. The result was that he found himself in as powerful a position as that enjoyed by his father, Zengi.

The result of this situation was that even Unur's death in November 1149 had no effect on the relationship between Damascus and Jerusalem. The following years saw the establishment of a contingent agreement that would come into force when Damascus was attacked by Nur al-Din. Thus, the Franks were informed when Nur al-Din headed toward Damascus in early 1150. He assured the Damascenes that he had been asked for help by the farmers and Bedouins in the region of Hawran, to the south of Damascus, and that he had no wish to harm the city. However, he did demand auxiliary troops and accused the Damascenes of being disloyal to the jihad. He appeared before the walls of the city in April 1150. This attack was spoiled by bad weather, but by the middle of May a peace agreement was reached according to which Damascus placed itself under Nur al-Din's overlordship. The beginning of May 1151 saw renewed hostilities, although Nur al-Din claimed that he was only interested in the jihad and in freeing captives held in Damascus. About a month later he was forced to retreat, as a Frankish army approached. At the end of July, Nur al-Din and Damascus once again made a peace agreement, and that autumn Damascus accepted his overlordship for a second time.

In early 1153, Nur al-Din planned an attack on the kingdom of Jerusalem in order to break the Frankish siege of Ascalon. This city was still under the control of the Fatimids in Egypt and represented their bridgehead into Syria. Therefore, the Damascene troops joined with Nur al-Din's soldiers, but the two sides came into conflict near Banyas with the result that the campaign had to be scuttled. The historian Ibn al-Athir ascribed Nur al-Din's final decision to capture Damascus to this failure. However, it should be noted that it was only in 1159 that Nur al-Din became interested in an anti-Frankish alliance with the Fatimids, first suggested by the latter in 1150. This was long after Ascalon had been captured by Baldwin III of Jerusalem in August 1153.

Nur al-Din developed an extensive jihad propaganda to accompany his expansionist designs on Damascus. He presented himself as the model warrior for the faith and sharply criticized the policies of the Damascene rulers regarding the kingdom of Jerusalem. It remains uncertain just how important this jihad propaganda really was in helping Nur al-Din finally to capture Damascus in 1154. Presumably, the decision by the city militia to lay down its arms was due far less to Nur al-Din's jihad propaganda than it was to the general unhappiness of the population with the rulers of the city and the economic difficulties that Damascus faced. The latter became particularly acute when Nur al-Din, who certainly did not rely on his propaganda alone, began, even before the beginning of the siege, to block grain shipments coming to the city from the north, thereby causing enormous price increases.

The End of the Syrian Balance of Power

The union of Damascus and Aleppo under Nur al-Din's rule had a decisive effect on political relations in Syria and meant the end of the Syrian tradition of maintaining a balance of power. According to Nur al-Din's propaganda, the conquest of Damascus was a precondition for the goal of reconquering Jerusalem and the Mediterranean coast. It is in this context that the 'Abbasid caliph al-Muqtafi is reported to have made Nur al-Din ruler of Egypt and the Crusader states in 1154 and to have ordered him to undertake their immediate conquest. But following his capture of Damascus, Nur al-Din was not primarily interested in undertaking the jihad against the Franks. Instead, the theme of the liberation of Jerusalem largely disappeared from his propaganda. As had been true of his father, Zengi, propagandizing the jihad against the Franks had served Nur al-Din by raising his prestige and consequently legitimizing his rule as well as his expansionist policies against Muslim neighbors. He maintained peaceful relations with the Franks as long as possible. He made a truce with Baldwin III of Jerusalem in May 1155 which was extended for a year in 1156 and included a provision that he pay tribute to Baldwin! War did not break out again until Frankish troops violated this agreement in the beginning of February 1157 by attacking Muslim farmers and herders in the neighborhood of Banyas. This war was presented as jihad in Nur al-

Din's propaganda. As a consequence, his army included volunteers who had only taken up arms to participate in the jihad.

In June 1157, Nur al-Din defeated Baldwin III's troops at Jacob's Ford on the Jordan River and took a large number of noble prisoners. However, the subsequent siege of Banyas had to be broken off when an earthquake in northern Syria severely damaged many of Nur al-Din's fortifications, thereby giving his opponents an invitation to attack. Aside from the Crusader states to the west, he was threatened to the north by Sultan Kilij Arslan II of the Rum-Seljuk empire of Konya, who was interested in cooperation with the Franks and the Armenians (of Cilicia).

In October 1157, following the repulse of an army from the Crusader states, Nur al-Din fell so ill that he named his younger brother Nusrat al-Din Amir Amiran as his successor in case of his own death. Reports of Nur al-Din's death led to a revolt in Aleppo by the majority Shi'ite population. The revolt collapsed, however, when it became clear that the ruler was still alive. The Franks also tried to use the situation to their advantage. Their siege of Shayzar failed as a result of a conflict concerning who would be the next ruler of the city. However, the Franks did succeed in capturing Harim at the beginning of February 1158. Nur al-Din, who recovered at about this time, felt compelled to seek revenge. But he suffered a major defeat in the summer of 1158 during his attack on the kingdom of Jerusalem.

Of much greater importance, however, is the fact that Baldwin III of Jerusalem, feeling threatened by the growth in Nur al-Din's power, sought a better relationship with the Byzantine emperor, Manuel Comnenus. The negotiations, begun in 1157, were sealed in 1158 with Baldwin's marriage to Manuel's niece Theodora. It seems likely that the two sides agreed to satisfy the Byzantine claims to Antioch, a matter that dated back to the First Crusade, and then to attack Nur al-Din.

The result was a Byzantine campaign in Cilicia and northern Syria in 1158–1159 that forced Reynald of Châtillon, the prince of Antioch, to take an oath of fealty to Manuel. In face of the Byzantine advance, Nur al-Din, who at this time again fell very ill, put the defenses of Aleppo in order and summoned his fellow believers to the jihad. However, the feared attack by the Byzantine and Frankish forces did not come to pass. Manuel saw that his goals had largely been achieved, and he entered into negotiations with

Nur al-Din, to the anger of his allies. The result was a truce and the release from captivity of a reported 6,000–10,000 prisoners from the Second Crusade held by Nur al-Din. When the latter attacked the Seljuk empire of Rum at the end of 1159 and beginning of 1160, to which his ambitious brother Nusrat al-Din had fled following his effort to foment rebellion during Nur al-Din's two bouts of illness, another element of the agreement reached with Manuel became clear. While Nur al-Din was launching his invasion, the emperor attacked the Seljuks of Rum on another front. In contrast to Nur al-Din, however, Manuel continued his campaign up to 1161 and finally won recognition of Byzantine overlordship by Sultan Kilij Arslan.

The Byzantine invasion of northern Syria secured the balance of power in the Near East for another decade. After his agreement with Manuel, Nur al-Din did not make any plans to attack the Crusader states for several years, despite the titles given to him in inscriptions on buildings he constructed from 1158 onward. The limited importance of these titles to practical politics is made clear by the fact that titles implying campaigns against Crusader states also were born by the rulers of Rum-Seljuk and the Artuqids, that is, by Nur al-Din's neighbors, who very seldom participated in the jihad against the Franks, if at all.

It was not Nur al-Din but rather the Fatimid vizier in Egypt who was particularly concerned with the struggle against the Franks and was seeking allies for this effort. Strikingly, Nur al-Din first demonstrated an interest in Fatimid proposals in 1158, and this was because of the agreement reached between Baldwin III and Manuel Comnenus. There was an exchange of several embassies, but after his agreement with the Byzantines in 1159, Nur al-Din no longer reacted to the admonitions from the Fatimid vizier to undertake the jihad against the Franks.

CHAPTER THREE

Saladin's Rise

Egypt as the Goal of Conquest

In 1158, Frankish emissaries tried in vain to negotiate a truce with Egypt. The Fatimid leadership nevertheless found itself, just a short time later, preparing to pay a yearly tribute to Jerusalem. The Fatimids did so, it seems, only to gain time to ready a major offensive. But the campaign never went beyond the planning stages because of the death of the vizier, Ibn Ruzzik, in 1161. When the Egyptians ended payment of the tribute, King Amalric of Jerusalem, the brother and successor of Baldwin III, used this as an excuse to attack, in September 1163, the strategically important city of Bilbays which was located along the route to Cairo. This attack failed, however, when the Egyptians pierced the dikes that were holding back the rising waters of the Nile and by this means flooded the country.

The struggle to succeed Ibn Ruzzik as Fatimid vizier, which was going on at this time, resulted in Egypt's being brought under Nur al-Din's control by the end of the decade. First, Shawar usurped the office of vizier in 1163. This same year, however, he had to give way to his rival Dirgham. Both of these men sought the support of Nur al-Din. In the end, Nur al-Din gave his support to Shawar. He sent troops to Egypt under the command of the one-eyed Kurdish emir Asad al-Din Shirkuh. They moved along the edge of the desert on the eastern border of the kingdom of Jerusalem heading toward Egypt. As a result, at the end of May 1164 Shawar became vizier for the second time. He then made clear that he would not fulfill the financial agreements that he had reached with Nur al-Din. He also refused to grant to the Syrian troops the lands that he had

promised as military fiefs. Instead, he ordered Shirkuh to leave the land of
the Nile. The result was a struggle between the former allies. Like his rival
Dirgham before, Shawar now requested aid from King Amalric of Jerusalem. In addition to promising a yearly tribute and the release of Christian prisoners, he also offered, as apparently Dirgham had done, to place
Egypt under the authority of the king of Jerusalem.

Clearly, Amalric had to hinder Nur al-Din from sending troops to
Egypt and thereby placing the kingdom of Jerusalem in a pincer. Shawar
is said to have stressed this danger when he made contact with the king.
The result of these discussions was the establishment of an agreement
between Amalric and Shawar. The two allies marched against Shirkuh at
Bilbays, where he had established his base of operations, and placed the
city under siege. Shawar apparently hoped to use this occasion to play the
Franks and the Syrians against each other. However, Amalric appears to
have had little interest in storming Bilbays. Therefore, after a siege lasting
several weeks, a peace agreement was reached in October 1164. According
to the terms, both Shirkuh and Amalric were required to leave Egypt,
perhaps also receiving a large sum of money from Shawar. For the time,
the latter had won.

While the military forces of the kingdom of Jerusalem were tied down
in Egypt, Nur al-Din used the opportunity to attack the Crusader states in
the north. He defeated the Franks in a pitched battle in August 1164 and
then recaptured the city of Harim, which had been taken from him in
1158. In October 1164, he succeeded in capturing the city of Banyas. This
success forced Amalric to leave Egypt. The victory also served as revenge
for a severe defeat that Nur al-Din had suffered in May 1163 when he was
surprised in his camp by his opponents at the foot of the Frankish fortress
of Crac de Chevaliers during an invasion of the county of Tripoli. He had
barely survived on this occasion. From a psychological perspective, this
defeat, which seemed to him a punishment inflicted by God, brought
about a major change in Nur al-Din's personality and caused him to adopt
a rigorous religious and ascetic style of life.

Nur al-Din did not originally plan to place the kingdom of Jerusalem in
a pincer through the conquest of Egypt. Following the failure of the first
campaign, it was less Nur al-Din than his ambitious emir Shirkuh who
planned a further intervention in Egypt. Apparently, Shirkuh saw the

conditions there as the chance of a lifetime to develop his own independent power.

Two years later Shirkuh began extensive preparations for a renewed campaign, with the support of Nur al-Din, and in January 1167 he set out a second time for Egypt. Amalric tried in vain to catch Shirkuh's army while it was on the march. When they had allied again, Amalric and Shawar were able to bring their opponent to battle, in March 1167. Up until then, Shirkuh, encamped on the western bank of the Nile, was unreachable. In the battle, the allies were defeated, but both sides suffered heavy losses. The victorious Shirkuh passed north of Cairo toward Alexandria, whose population opened the gates to him and provided him with substantial support. Despite the defeat they had suffered, Amalric and Shawar remained capable of maneuver and attempted to starve Alexandria into submission by imposing a blockade on land as well as on water. This blockade forced Shirkuh, along with the greater part of his troops, to leave Alexandria and head south toward upper Egypt, so that he would not lose his own ability to maneuver. He also hoped to increase the strength of his army by recruiting Bedouins. He placed his nephew Salah al-Din Yusuf, known still in the West as Saladin, in command of the troops left behind to defend Alexandria.

In view of this situation, Amalric and Shawar decided to impose a regular siege on the city. This was a hard test for Saladin, who had already participated in Shirkuh's first Egyptian campaign. In July 1167, following a three-month blockade, Alexandria was low on food supplies. Nevertheless, Saladin's troops, supported by the population of the city, warded off all attacks, despite great suffering. During this period, Shirkuh remained militarily passive and did not undertake even a relief attack on Cairo, which was defended by a Frankish garrison. Instead, there were negotiations, which led, in August 1167, to a peace agreement. In return for the surrender of Alexandria to Shawar, Shirkuh received free departure for all of his troops to Syria and an amnesty for the population of Alexandria. The terms also included an exchange of all prisoners and the payment of money by Shawar to both Amalric and Shirkuh.

It would appear that during these negotiations, the opponents also had a chance to get to know each other on a personal level. At Amalric's invitation, Saladin spent several days in the Frankish camp. The king granted Saladin's request that his sick and wounded troops be spared a journey over land and instead be carried by ship to Acre, from where they could be transported to Damascus. Saladin also asked Amalric to ensure that Shawar would keep the agreement, which he at first had violated, to grant an amnesty to the people of Alexandria. A quarter-century later, participants in the Third Crusade even said that Saladin had struck up a friendship with Humphrey II of Toron, the constable of the kingdom of Jerusalem, who dubbed him a knight.

Before Shirkuh and Amalric left the field for a second time, in August 1167, following the terms of their agreement, still further arrangements were made. Shawar agreed to pay a large annual tribute to the Franks and even accepted the establishment of a Frankish garrison in Cairo. These troops were to see to the punctual payment of the money and also to guard the city gates. Shawar, who, in contrast to the situation in 1164, could not feel that he was the victor in 1167, preferred a "protectorate" under the Frankish Christians to the protection offered by the Syrian Muslims. Undoubtedly, the dangers of this policy were clear to him, and Shirkuh is reported to have implored him to make common cause with the Syrians against the Franks for the advantage of Islam. However, as Shirkuh and his emirs were aware, the Egyptians, with the exception of the people of Alexandria, were opposed to them. This was true despite the fact that the majority of the population living under the rule of the Isma'ili Shi'ite Fatimids were Sunni Muslims, like the Turkish and Kurdish troops of Nur al-Din. Most of the Egyptian sources called the latter "*Ghuzz*," a term that was originally used to designate the non-Muslim Turks who lived on the borders of the Islamic world. Perhaps in the view of the Isma'ili minority who decided Egyptian policy, as in the eyes of the Shi'ites in general, the jihad against non-Shi'ite Muslims, such as the Sunni, was more important than the jihad against the Christians.

Nevertheless, the agreement reached between Shawar and Amalric did arouse the displeasure of the Fatimid caliph, as well as the inhabitants of Cairo. Shawar's own son, al-Kamil, joined a conspiracy that was not only directed against Shawar but was also intended to bring about the destruction of the Fatimid caliphate. The conspirators asked Nur al-Din to restore law and order in Egypt and to reunite the strength of Islam. They offered to pay a yearly tribute, and they sent a large sum of money to Nur al-Din when he gave them a positive response. In this context, a rumor reached Jerusalem that Saladin and al-Kamil wished to marry each other's sisters. If that were not enough, the participants in a different plot, also directed against Shawar, sought the support of Amalric. Shawar thus found himself in an exceptionally dangerous situation. He put to death a whole series of suspected opponents, including many who apparently were innocent, and promised financial rewards to Nur al-Din if the sultan could disrupt Shirkuh's plans regarding Egypt. Although Nur al-Din signaled to the conspirators around al-Kamil his readiness to intervene again in Egyptian affairs, he sent word to Shawar in the summer of 1168 that he had named Shirkuh governor of Hims and that the income associated with the position had convinced Shirkuh to give up his plans regarding Egypt.

Nevertheless, just half a year later, Shirkuh marched into Egypt for the third time. In contrast to his earlier campaigns, on this occasion he was reacting to actions taken by the king of Jerusalem. The latter, under pressure from the order of St. John, the Pisans, and a group of vassals, decided to invade the land of the Nile once again. After he made Nur al-Din think that he intended to attack the city of Hims in northern Syria and thereby gained a head start, Amalric led his army south from Ascalon on 20 October 1168. Without slowing his march, he sent on ahead several different explanations to Shawar that were intended to reassure him. By 4 November, he had already captured the strategically important city of Bilbays, whose population was massacred by Amalric's troops. This action was an important factor in the subsequent bitter defensive struggle by the Egyptians when the Franks departed Bilbays a short time later heading for Cairo and Fustat. The latter had been replaced as the capital of Egypt by the Fatimids in 969 in favor of Cairo, which was built just to the north.

Shawar at first hoped to stall Amalric's attack by quickly mobilizing troops at Bilbays. When this effort failed and the Franks marched deeper into Egyptian territory, he burned Fustat because he did not think that it was possible to defend the old capital and he wanted to keep Amalric from using it as a base of operations for attacking Cairo. Amalric demonstrated that he was not impressed by Shawar's actions, and promptly attacked Cairo, where the population of Fustat in the meantime had taken refuge. However, he was not successful in capturing the caliph's city, either by storm or through a siege of several weeks. Instead, there were again negotiations, in the course of which Shawar declared he would pay an immediate sum of 100,000 dinars, and several times this amount later on, if Amalric gave up his siege of Cairo. As soon as the king had received the smaller sum, he retreated north and left the vicinity of Cairo.

As the Franks went from being allies to being enemies, Egyptian propaganda changed as well. Shawar was celebrated as a defender of the faith and urged by the poet 'Umara al-Yamani to protect Islam from the unbelieving Franks. In addition, a call for jihad against the Franks that likely was composed at this time appealed to two Bedouin tribes that had always been unreliable.

Amalric's attack on Egypt wrecked Shawar's policy. However, it was apparently not until Frankish troops appeared before Cairo in mid-November that the Fatimid caliph al-'Adid asked Nur al-Din for aid. Despite Shawar's warnings, al-'Adid preferred, at least in this situation, an alliance with a (Sunni) Muslim over an alliance with a (Frankish) Christian. The situation also makes clear that Nur al-Din was prepared to intervene, although at that time he was busy with other plans.

After Nur al-Din had used Amalric's absence in 1167 to launch an attack on Tripoli, without, however, gaining any real advantages, his attention in 1168 was directed primarily to the situation developing in the east of his kingdom. There, after a long siege and through an exchange of properties, he succeeded, on 26 October, in obtaining the fortress of Qal'at Ja'bar, which was considered unassailable. It guarded one of the most important crossing points over the Euphrates River and now secured Nur al-Din's connection to Mosul. Nevertheless, he reacted immediately when he learned, earlier that same month, shortly after the beginning of Amalric's campaign, that the Franks had marched toward Egypt. The request for aid from Cairo did not reach him until after he had already begun preparations for a campaign in Egypt. He once more entrusted command of this campaign to Shirkuh. The latter insisted on being accompanied again by his nephew Saladin, who apparently took no joy in this distinction and participated very unwillingly, as he remembered the difficult fighting he had experienced in Egypt.

In mid-December, Shirkuh set out with his army from Ra's al-Ma'. When Amalric found out, he immediately set out for the city of Bilbays, which he had captured several weeks before. He used it as his base of operations to try to catch Shirkuh's troops during their march through the desert of the Sinai. Accompanied by several thousand prisoners of both sexes from Bilbays, whom he later sold as slaves, Amalric left Egypt in the beginning of 1169. The caliph al-'Adid had achieved his goal, but several days later Shirkuh's army appeared before Cairo. Now that Shawar had no opportunity to play one opponent off against another, and as vizier had lost the support of the caliph, the gates of Cairo were finally open to Shirkuh. Soon thereafter, al-'Adid summoned Shirkuh to an audience. Despite being accompanied by his bodyguards, Shawar was taken prisoner on 18 January 1169 by Saladin. This action may have been precipitated by Shawar's own plan to arrest Shirkuh during a banquet. Shawar then was killed at the caliph's command. On the next day, al-'Adid named Shirkuh vizier and commander of the Egyptian troops. Shirkuh then assigned administrative responsibilities to Saladin.

In public, Nur al-Din received news of Shirkuh's successes with approval, but in reality he had mixed feelings. He probably would have preferred to see Shirkuh and his troops back in Syria. Shirkuh, however, had very little time to enjoy his power and fame. Well-known for his tendency toward gluttony, he died on 23 March 1169 following an exceptionally rich meal. William of Tyre, who rose several years later to serve as chancellor of the kingdom of Jerusalem and archbishop of Tyre, characterized Shirkuh, in his history of the kings of Jerusalem, as a man of small stature, corpulent but full of a desire for fame. He bore every burden, including hunger and thirst, to achieve his aims. He was very generous and beloved by his troops. He was not only capable in arms and experienced in war but also educated and eloquent.

Seizing Power

Shirkuh's successor as vizier and commander of the Egyptian and Syrian troops was his nephew Saladin. Although there were four other, older emirs (three Kurds and one Turk) among Nur al-Din's troops who hoped for the office of vizier, Saladin quickly obtained the support of the Kurdish emirs. He may have been the compromise candidate, having been chosen by Shirkuh as commander of the Syrian troops, although he does not appear to have actively sought the office. The decision led to an open dispute as a result of which some of Nur al-Din's Turkish troops went back to Syria. The Fatimid caliph may have hoped for just this outcome when he named Saladin vizier on 26 March 1169. He allegedly thought that Saladin had a weaker position than the other candidates and therefore chose him. In contrast to a faction of his advisors, the caliph did not seriously consider an Egyptian for this office.

Very little is known about Saladin's youth and family background. Born in Tikrit in 1138, he grew up in Baalbek and received his first posts in Aleppo and Damascus. Aside from his military training, and his eager participation in polo, which served to sharpen his riding skills, he likely had a knowledge of theology and law. In addition, following Arab tradition, he was also probably familiar with the genealogies, history, and poetry of the Arabs. In the view of his paternal family members, Saladin was Kurdish only on his mother's side but had Arab blood from his father's family. His father Najm al-Din Ayyub and his uncle Asad al-Din Shirkuh were political adventurers. Both brothers came from Armenia and sought their fortune first in Iraq and then in Syria. Several times, but not always together, they changed lords and did not shrink from betraying them. Once they entered Nur al-Din's service, Ayyub's position as governor of Damascus and Shirkuh's command of the army provided the foundation for Saladin's rise.

Saladin went by his proper name (Ar. *ism*), Yusuf, during his life. In contrast to Ayyub and Shirkuh, however, he has passed into history under his honorific name. Very early on he also was compared by his contemporaries to Joseph of Egypt, Jacob's son from the Old Testament. As was true of Joseph, he brought his father and brothers to Egypt and gave them land. His elder brother, Turanshah, with other members of the Ayyubid family, arrived in Cairo at the end of July 1169. His father followed in mid-April 1170. In an unusual event, Ayyub was met before the gates of the city by al-'Adid and personally greeted. More family members came later, probably in February 1171. Politically very experienced and so favored by Nur al-Din that he was not required to stand in the presence of the sultan, Ayyub remained an important advisor to Saladin until his death in the summer of 1173 following a riding accident. When Saladin's ambitious brothers and nephews took over military offices, his duties became much more manageable.

Saladin quickly determined how to secure his position. He began to reorganize internal Egyptian affairs by first undermining the existing Egyptian institutions and then replacing them step by step. He started with the reorganization of the Egyptian army, because he had no real control over the Fatimid troops, who considerably outnumbered his own. He established new units and built them up around a central core of his own bodyguard. At the same time Saladin weakened the Fatimid units. He stripped the commanders of the lands that had been granted to them by the caliph, and then granted these lands to his new troops as military fiefs (*iqta'*). In return for the revenues from these lands, the possessors had to provide personal military service and troops, as well as ensure the cultivation of the property and the maintenance of the irrigation systems. There were also military fiefs that did not involve a grant of land. The possessors of such fiefs received income from nonagricultural taxes and sometimes were assigned revenues from tax farms. Thus, for example, Saladin's father received as his military fief a portion of the tax income from the port cities of Alexandria and Damietta.

Because of the Nile, Egypt had always been an economically wealthy and administratively sophisticated land. However, despite centuries of Muslim rule, many important administrative duties were not in the hands of Muslims but rather were held by the members of the still numerous Coptic population and, in some cases, by Jews. Saladin, whose father was placed in charge of the treasury by the caliph and, thus, was in charge of Egypt's finances, did not change this system at all. Admittedly, in 1172, he ordered that all non-Muslims be stripped of their offices, but this order was not put into effect. Presumably, this move was meant for propaganda purposes alone, since Saladin could not make any significant changes without endangering his well-functioning system. The Copts were not necessarily entirely loyal to the Fatimids, although they had faced few difficulties under their rule; and they never did cooperate with the Franks of the Crusader states, a situation that would have been very threatening to the Muslims.

In March 1171, following the death of the incumbent chancellor, Saladin placed the chancery under the control of a Sunni Muslim, al-Qadi al-Fadil, the hunchbacked son of a judge from Ascalon. While in the service of the Fatimids he had already held several posts and, among other documents, had composed the texts naming Shirkuh and then Saladin as vizier. Within a short time, he became famous as a stylist and master of rhymed prose. Over the next two decades, he proved himself as a tireless worker and one of Saladin's most important advisors.

In the second year of his vizierate, after withstanding the first periods of turbulence, Saladin put into effect a series of politico-religious desires that, in accordance with the majority Sunni population of Egypt, were directed at the Isma'ili-Shi'ite beliefs of the Fatimids. The Shi'ite call to prayer "come to the best deed" could no longer be heard from any minaret. In addition to the fourth caliph, Ali, the names of his three predecessors, Abu Bakr, 'Umar, and 'Uthman, were again heard at the Friday prayer. In the Sunni view, all four of these caliphs were "rightly guided." In this context, it is striking that Saladin named his oldest son, born in June 1170, 'Ali, the name of the caliph particularly honored by the Shi'ites. By contrast, in 1171, the year in which the Fatimid caliphate was suppressed, Saladin named his second son 'Uthman, the name of the caliph who was particularly hated by the Shi'ites.

Above all, Saladin strengthened Sunni Islam in Egypt through the foundation of theological law schools (Ar. singular, *madrasa*) in Cairo and Fustat, one of the Malikite tradition and one of the Shafi'ite. He followed this in March 1171 with the replacement of the highest-ranking Egyptian judge. Saladin replaced him with a Sunni, a legal scholar of Shafi'ite tradition and Kurdish origin, who saw to it that all legal positions in Egypt were filled with Sunni Muslims, particularly ones with Shafi'ite training. In April 1171, Saladin's nephew Taqi al-Din 'Umar established a Shafi'ite madrasa, too. In the following years, additional schools were founded. Saladin made clear, in this process, that he particularly favored the Shafi'ite tradition among the four Sunni legal schools. The grave of the famous jurist al-Shafi'i (died 820), which was located very near to Fustat, was especially venerated by Saladin and his family.

In the view of the Shi'ites, it was permitted and even encouraged to refrain from openly declaring one's religious views while living under Sunni rule. Rather, Shi'ites were to hide their true beliefs and live as Sunnis among the Sunnis. As a result, special measures were required to control the adherents of the Fatimids. To this end, Saladin used the already existing office of the muhtasib, a learned jurist whose task it was to watch over the customs and practices of the market. As al-Shayzari wrote

in a book commissioned by Saladin regarding the institution of the *hisba*, it was the duty of the muhtasib to take action against the many heretical novelties and sects, because they hindered the establishment of Islamic law in Egypt.

When considering what was necessary for the maintenance of public order, Saladin could turn to his own experience as police chief of Damascus, where his father had been governor. In a poem written at that time, thieves were warned about him. He apparently acted harshly toward lawbreakers. In some cases he even went beyond his jurisdiction, and consequently many of his decisions were ruled invalid according to Islamic law by the judge of Damascus.

As had been the case with Nur al-Din before 1163, Saladin in his younger years did not live a particularly model life. However, according to his biographer Baha' al-Din Ibn Shaddad, Saladin gave up drinking wine and other pleasures when he became vizier. It is likely that it was at this point that he also married for the first time. In any case, it was only in June 1170 that his first son, al-Afdal 'Ali, was born. Then, at almost yearly intervals, further sons followed from three other wives. As the example of the Roman emperor Titus, among others, shows, over the course of history radical changes in lifestyle can frequently be seen to accompany the taking control of the reins of government.

At about the same time he decided to give up drinking, Saladin abolished the tax on the brewing of *mizr*, a type of beer, and apparently also eliminated the tax on wine. These actions might be seen as encouragement of vices that completely contradicted the Islamic prohibition on wine and alcohol, in general. Nevertheless, apparently through the urging of Saladin's father, Ayyub, the sale of wine continued to be permitted in Alexandria, because many Italian merchants lived there.

Although it was Egypt's wealth that permitted Saladin to carry out his ongoing wars, in his later years, he wrote in a letter to al-Qadi al-Fadil, to the latter's outrage, that Egypt in his eyes was nothing but a whore who tried in vain to keep him separated from Syria, his true wife. This was particularly insulting given Saladin's struggle against prostitution. It is not until 1178 and 1179 that we learn that Saladin shut down the brothels in Egypt and threw prostitutes into prison. By contrast, Christian sources in Latin from the time of the Third Crusade accuse Saladin of having obtained taxes from prostitutes at the beginning of his career (as police chief) and then of having used the money to make himself beloved by the population of Damascus by putting on public entertainments.

Soon after the end of the Fatimid caliphate in September 1171, internal tariffs (Ar. *mukus*) were ended, because they were not permitted under Islamic law. This was not only a demonstration of a return to true Islam but also served to strengthen trade. No less important from the point of view of propaganda, Saladin presented himself as social benefactor by establishing central control over the collection of the alms tax (Ar. *zakat*). Up to this point, in Egypt each Muslim had decided for himself which needy people or pious institutions he would support with his alms. Saladin's reforms allowed him to make good the financial losses caused by the abolition of the internal tariffs. The alms tax was used by his government not only to support social causes but also to pay for other projects, such as the costs of the Egyptian fleet in 1191. In a practice criticized by Ibn Jubayr, a traveler from Andalusia, this alms tax was imposed on pilgrims to Mecca as well, albeit apparently without Saladin's knowledge. Many of the taxes that Saladin abolished were revived by his successors as a consequence of the continually increasing costs of war. Indeed, some of the taxes may have been revived by Saladin himself. They also revived the taxes imposed on alcohol and other sins. In 1193, shortly after Saladin's death, his son al-ʿAziz ʿUthman also lacked money. It remains unclear when and why Saladin went back on the decisions he had made earlier in his reign to reintroduce one particular rule, which had not been enforced under the Fatimids, namely that non-Muslims had to pay a double toll.

The first challenge to Saladin's reign developed in August 1169 when a conspiracy against him was uncovered. The conspirators made plans with the king of Jerusalem, who was to renew his attack on Egypt in conjunction with the Byzantines. Saladin was able to lull into complacency the leader of the conspiracy, a black eunuch who possessed considerable power in his role as a major domo in the caliph's palace. However, when the man left Cairo to inspect his property in the countryside, Saladin had him arrested and killed, and then replaced him with one of his own loyal supporters. In response, the large and powerful units of black slaves decided to raise a revolt, and they were joined by the Armenian guard. Saladin and his brother Turanshah were able to put down the rebellion only after two days of brutal fighting. As a result of this battle, the Fatimid caliphate lost all of its military strength, although the following years did witness numerous battles between Saladin's troops and black rebels in upper Egypt.

At the end of 1169, Saladin also had to fend off an attack by a Byzantine fleet and a Frankish land army against the port city of Damietta. The attack was planned in 1168 following Amalric's marriage to a Byzantine princess in August 1167. Amalric did not set out with his army toward Egypt until the middle of October 1168, despite the fact that the Byzantine fleet had been ready for action for several weeks. It appears that Amalric wanted to wait until the end of the annual Nile flood, caused by the yearly rains in the Ethiopian highlands, which covered broad sections of Egypt with layers of nutrient-rich mud up through November. In this way, Amalric hoped to correct the error that had forced him to retreat from Egypt in 1163. However, the Byzantines at Damietta experienced supply problems and their fleet was not able to cut off Damietta's line of communication by way of the Nile, so the only means of capturing the city was by storm. When this attack failed, the siege of the city was ended in mid-December with a formulaic peace agreement.

The Franks did not participate in the final assault on the walls of Damietta, and the Byzantines therefore accused them of secretly carrying on negotiations with the Muslims and of purposefully delaying a decisive action for this reason. However, as Saladin informed Frederick Barbarossa sometime in the period 1171–1173, it was the Byzantines who had sought to make secret contact with their opponents behind the backs of their allies. During the battle for Damietta, Saladin remained at Cairo. Apparently fearing that there would be another revolt, he had numerous leading Egyptians put to death. Nur al-Din was suspicious, too. Despite a request by the Fatimid caliph, following the end of the siege of Damietta, he did not withdraw the Syrian troops whom he had sent in July to Saladin and his brother Turanshah to defend against the expected attack.

The Collapse of the Fatimid Caliphate

A year and a half later, in June 1171, Nur al-Din ordered Saladin to forbid the name of the Fatimid caliph to be said during the Friday sermon

(Ar. *khutba*) in the mosques in Egypt. Instead, the name of the 'Abbasid caliph was to be used. Thus, he demanded the official return of Egypt to Sunni Islam and, at the same time, the end of 202 years of Fatimid rule. In this manner, Nur al-Din, who proceeded vigorously against the Shi'ites in Syria, not only would appear as a champion of Sunni orthodoxy and be able naturally to count on the approval of the 'Abbasid caliph in Baghdad, but also could hope to force Saladin, who as the servant of two masters had been difficult to control, into a more dependent role. Saladin may perhaps have been hesitant to carry out Nur al-Din's commands, but he did so—after preparing the groundwork. First, he ensured the support of the Sunni jurists, whose legal decisions provided the expected approval for the removal of the Fatimid caliph. In addition, he had a number of Egyptian emirs, who could have posed a threat to his position, arrested and their property confiscated. The completion of his preparations was marked by a large military parade, which he held at Cairo on 11 September 1171 as a demonstration of his power to intimidate all of his potential opponents.

The Fatimid caliphate came to an end shortly after the beginning of the new Islamic year 567. However, the timing may have had less to do with the calendar than with the illness of Caliph al-'Adid, which was so severe that he died after about two weeks, on the night of 12–13 September. The possibility cannot be excluded that he was poisoned. However, despite the claims of Christian sources, it is not likely that Saladin was guilty of the death of the twenty-year-old caliph. After an apparent bid to gauge public reaction through a test run in the main mosque of Fustat on 10 September, the first Friday of the year 567, the Friday sermon in both Cairo and Fustat on 17 September 1171 was held in the name of the 'Abbasid caliph. After the event, several of the men in attendance who were from outside Egypt praised this as a courageous act. It speaks to the success of Saladin's preparations that there were no immediate armed reactions and not even protests from the supporters of the Fatimids to the events of 17 September. Many of them appear to have left the city, because after these events they felt safer in the countryside. The return of Egypt to Sunni Islam was sealed by the minting of Egyptian coins in December that had the name of the 'Abbasid caliph al-Mustadi on one side and the name of Nur al-Din on the other.

When news arrived about the end of Fatimid rule in Egypt, the 'Abbasid caliph in Baghdad did not hesitate to grant Nur al-Din the rule over Syria and Egypt. Dressed in the wide, long-sleeved robe of honor made from silk that the caliph had given to him, Nur al-Din rode through the streets of Damascus, leading a second horse by the reins, under the black banner of the 'Abbasids and then held a military parade. Saladin also wore a robe of honor from Baghdad as he rode on a March day in 1172 through the streets of Cairo, to present himself to the population of the city.

At Saladin's order, the members of the Fatimid ruling family were taken prisoner. After the separation of men and women from each other, they could produce no further heirs, and their family was thus condemned to die out. The famed Fatimid library also suffered a sad fate. Saladin did not have the rich collections burned, despite their heretical content, but he did not keep them; and over the following years multivolume works were sold off book by book, auctioned to canny dealers at prices far below their value.

Al-'Adid remained the last Fatimid caliph. He was not responsible for the end of his dynasty, as he was only very occasionally the master of his own decisions. His predecessors had already lost a great part of their power to their viziers. One consequence of the continuous intrigue among the various interest groups at the caliphal court was that the viziers frequently changed, and, as a rule, did not die a natural death. In addition to the court's lack of inner stability, the weakening of the military played an important role in bringing the Fatimid period to an end. The vizier Dirgham, in the course of his struggle to gain power in 1163, killed dozens of the highest ranking and most experienced officers of the Fatimid army during a banquet, in an effort to nip in the bud a conspiracy directed against him.

After he pushed the Fatimids aside, Saladin still had not overcome all of the internal Egyptian resistance to his rule. The quiet of 1171 was deceptive. In March 1174, he became aware of a plot that was intended to bring the Fatimid rulers back to power with the support of the king of Jerusalem. Various groups belonged to this conspiracy, including men who had lost positions and incomes. These were by no means all Isma'ilis but included Sunni emirs and Saladin's soldiers as well. The leaders of this conspiracy were crucified in Cairo in April, including the respected Sunni poet 'Umara al-Yamani.

He is a good example of how little the jihad-propaganda in court poetry of the twelfth century was marked by deep conviction. As a Fatimid court poet, who was usually paid for his works, 'Umara first composed poems in praise of jihad on behalf of the vizier Ibn Ruzzik, as well as for his successors al-Nasir Ruzzik and Dirgham. While Shawar was vizier, 'Umara supported the alliance with Amalric. It was only in the aftermath of the Frankish attack on Egypt in 1168 that he again wrote poetry in favor of jihad and celebrated Shawar as a champion of Islam. After the latter's death, he celebrated the soldiers of Nur al-Din and Saladin. Finally, he took part in the 1174 conspiracy. A similar example of political flexibility can be seen in the case of al-Qadi al-Fadil, another Sunni at the Fatimid court, who rose to be chief of the Fatimid chancery under al-'Adid. In his poetry, he first praised the Fatimids and condemned, in a corresponding manner, the 'Abbasid caliphs at Baghdad. However, as a supporter of Saladin he reversed himself completely.

Military and Diplomatic Activities

Although Saladin followed Nur al-Din's command to end the Fatimid rule, the next two years saw the development of tensions between the two men that made it appear ever more likely that there would be an armed confrontation. For Nur al-Din, who had never been in Egypt and was not familiar with the conditions there, the limited military and financial assistance that Saladin offered to him to carry out his own plans must have seemed particularly annoying even if Saladin's claim that he was not in a position to begin any major undertakings using Egyptian resources was true.

It was in this context that Saladin began his military action against the kingdom of Jerusalem with the highly promising capture of Ayla in the winter of 1170–1171. In the hands of the Franks, Ayla represented a standing threat to the caravan route between Cairo and Damascus as well as the one between Cairo and Mecca. In addition, through their possession of Ayla, the Franks had secured their own route to the Red Sea, which was exceptionally important for the Egyptian trade with India. But Saladin's success in this case may well have made Nur al-Din suspect, in view of the well-known ambition of the Ayyubid family, that Saladin was less interested in the struggle against the Franks than he was in establishing in the region of the Dead Sea and the Sinai a buffer zone between himself and Nur al-Din that would keep the latter from interfering directly in Egyptian affairs.

Shortly after the removal of the Fatimids, without expecting any possible negative consequences, Saladin proceeded with his planned action against the Franks. At the end of September or the beginning of October 1171, he appeared with his army before the powerful Frankish fortress of Montréal (Shawbak). This was located south of the Dead Sea on the route from Cairo to Damascus. Together with the Frankish fortress of Karak to the north, it controlled the communications between Egypt and Syria. It is unclear whether Saladin was following an order issued by Nur al-Din to participate in a joint operation against the Franks, or whether Nur al-Din joined in only after he learned that Saladin had begun his campaign. Both scenarios are possible, because Nur al-Din had undertaken a brief action against Karak in April 1170 and, therefore, was aware of the strengths and weaknesses of the fortress. In any case, Saladin broke off his siege of Montréal as Nur al-Din approached Karak with his own troops. He avoided any personal meeting with Nur al-Din and turned back toward Egypt. Clearly, he preferred to see the fortresses of Karak and Montréal in the hands of the Franks rather than in the hands of a dangerously close Nur al-Din. Apparently, however, Saladin had suffered a defeat at the hands of Bedouins, who were allied with the Franks, and lost part of his baggage train. He excused himself to Nur al-Din with the reasonable explanation that difficulties in Egypt required his return to the Nile.

Saladin's operations in the Karak region in the summer of 1173 appear not to have been directed against the fortification itself. Rather, they were a reaction to the defeat suffered at the hands of the Bedouins from that region in 1171. The explanation for Saladin's decision to break off this campaign before achieving any success is likely to be found in the riding accident that cost Saladin's father his life nine days later. Ayyub was first buried in Cairo alongside Shirkuh. However, both brothers' final resting place, to which they were moved two years later, was in Medina, where, in addition to the Prophet Muhammad, many pious Muslims were buried. Ayyub and Shirkuh had each undertaken a pilgrimage as leader of the yearly Syrian pilgrim caravan, the former in 1157 and the latter in 1161.

The death of the always circumspect Ayyub, whom Nur al-Din had sent to Egypt in 1170 in an apparent effort to ensure that Saladin would follow his orders, may well have increased Nur al-Din's distrust of Saladin.

Saladin was not only active against the kingdom of Jerusalem in this period. The troops of his nephew Taqi al-Din 'Umar, whose ranks included many adventurers, helped to expand his power to the west in 1173 beyond the cities of Barqa and Tripoli up to the borders of the powerful Almohad empire. For reasons that are unclear, at the end of February 1174, Saladin's brother Turanshah set out to conquer Yemen. In view of the weakening of the military forces that he had available in Egypt, one might well ask whether Saladin did not expect an attack by Nur al-Din, or whether he calmly awaited such an attack. Perhaps he wished to know that Turanshah was busily engaged outside of Egypt because he feared the latter's ambition. Perhaps Turanshah was interested in establishing his own rule in Yemen. Among other places, he conquered the cities of Zabid, San'a, and Aden. He had the Friday prayer said again in the name of the 'Abbasid caliph, as Saladin had stressed in his letters that he should. Thus, in these regions, the earlier Egyptian overlordship, which had been achieved under the Fatimids, was now reestablished. Finally, it was of more than minor importance that these campaigns kept the Ayyubid troops occupied and provided a means to pay them. The constant effort to expand became the basis and hallmark of Saladin's rule.

Undoubtedly, Saladin made considerable public efforts to keep Nur al-Din informed about all of his activities and plans and included, as well, an appropriate level of self-praise. The campaigns in North Africa and Yemen, of which Nur al-Din approved, certainly could not be kept secret. It was otherwise with the diplomatic ties that Saladin pursued. He did not hesitate to accept Frederick Barbarossa's offer of an alliance in the period around 1171–1173. He sent a representative to the emperor, who is reported to have emphasized Saladin's commitment to keeping agreements and his love of the truth in contrast to the double-dealing of the Byzantines. Probably as a way of masking these friendly communications with an enemy of the faith, it was recorded in Germany that Saladin had asked for the hand of the emperor's daughter on behalf of his son, and had promised in return that he and all of his followers would convert to Christianity and set free all of his Christian prisoners. The agreement reached with Barbarossa apparently was directed against the Byzantines, who were also interested in good relations with Saladin. However, Saladin did not return their interest. Soon after this, Saladin appears also to have reached an agreement with Pisa, in order to ward off an attack that a fleet from Norman Sicily was undertaking against Alexandria in 1174.

We know nothing about a possible consultation by Saladin with Nur al-Din in regard to either agreement. As Barbarossa's initiative shows, the Christians thought of Saladin as a sovereign ruler of Egypt and independent of Nur al-Din. This view is made clear in William of Tyre's description of Saladin, shortly after the end of the Fatimid caliphate, as *calipha et soldanus*, that is as both caliph and vizier. Moreover, the goal of King Amalric's request for a new crusade, which he sent to Europe in 1173, was to ward off not only the threat posed by Nur al-Din but also the threatening power of Saladin.

Barbarossa and Saladin made contact again in 1175 when, in September, an imperial representative named Burchard sailed from Genoa to Egypt and from there journeyed to Syria, where, in the meantime, Saladin had gone to fight for Nur al-Din's inheritance. Burchard composed a description of the land and people, preserved in Arnold of Lübeck's *Slavic Chronicle*, which contained very little of the kind of prejudice toward Islam that was widely disseminated in the West during this period. Burchard was impressed by the wealth of Egypt. Unfortunately, however, he did not mention the goal or result of his mission. Presumably, he was supposed to congratulate Saladin on his most recent successes and find out Saladin's intentions.

In contrast to the Christians, the Muslim historians have nothing to say about Saladin's relations with Barbarossa. Perhaps they did not consider these worth mentioning because they did not end up producing any concrete results. On the other hand, perhaps the connection with Barbarossa seemed too compromising. Thus, the most interesting instructions of Saladin for his ambassador Abu Tahir Isma'il are not to be found in a chronicle but significantly in an Arabic collection of the letters of al-Qadi al-Fadil.

CHAPTER FOUR

Nur al-Din's Inheritance

Nur al-Din's Final Years

Nur al-Din apparently was unaware of Saladin's diplomatic activities. At the very least, he mistrusted Saladin's handling of Egyptian finances. Shirkuh's three campaigns to Egypt had imposed costs that had to be paid for. On several occasions, Saladin sent coined money to Syria. However, the greater part of the wealth that he sent consisted of precious objects from the Fatimid treasury, which were of little value in Nur al-Din's view. The size of the sums of coined money sent by Saladin must have been particularly disappointing to Nur al-Din. Egypt at that time had the reputation of being a land filled with treasure, whose reserves of gold were thought to be inexhaustible, but the supplies of gold had declined as the gold mines and the tombs of the pharaohs were exhausted. In Saladin's defense, it must be emphasized that the lavish household expenses of the Fatimids and the payments that Shawar had made to the Franks had severely depleted the Fatimid treasury by the time Saladin took power. In addition, Saladin's efforts at reorganization, which also were carried out in Nur al-Din's interest, at least in the short term, were very expensive.

On the other hand, the renewed strength of Egypt increased Saladin's own power, too, and this posed a danger to Nur al-Din. As a result of this situation, in the winter of 1173–1174 or sometime early in the latter year, Nur al-Din made a clear demonstration of his lack of confidence in Saladin by sending one of his own confidants to Cairo. This man was to audit the Egyptian finances, which earlier had been overseen by Ayyub, and to establish the size of the money payments that Saladin was required to send. As a consequence, Saladin issued a report, and sent one of his own envoys to deliver it to Damascus. In the meantime, Nur al-Din prepared for a major campaign, which Ibn al-Athir reported was directed against Egypt. Thus, an invasion of Egypt by Nur al-Din was certainly in the offing just before his death, on 15 May 1174, removed this danger to Saladin.

In the period after Shirkuh's conquest of Egypt, Nur al-Din did not remain silent on the question of freeing Jerusalem from the hands of the Franks, and, indeed, presented this undertaking as his most important political goal. In this context, a pulpit (Ar. *minbar*) was built in Aleppo at his order, to be installed in the Aqsa Mosque after the capture of the holy city. In addition, he had himself celebrated, in letters and poems that were sent to the caliph in Baghdad, as a champion of Islam in the jihad against the Franks.

Despite this self-presentation, Nur al-Din continued to expand his power at the expense of his Muslim neighbors, whom he occasionally attacked in military campaigns. After the death of his brother Qutb al-Din Mawdud in September 1170, Nur al-Din interjected himself in the decision about the succession in Mosul. In January 1171, following the accession of his younger nephew Sayf al-Din Ghazi, Nur al-Din gained recognition of his overlordship. The Friday prayer was already said in his name and had been for several years. Sayf al-Din married a daughter of Nur al-Din. Then, at the command of the latter, Sayf al-Din ordered that all taxes contrary to Islamic law be abolished and that the taxes imposed on Christians be raised. Nur al-Din's plan to attack the principality of Antioch, in conjunction with Kilij Arslan II of Konya, who was the sultan of the Rum-Seljuks and a brother of one of Nur al-Din's wives, collapsed when Kilij Arslan withdrew from the planned offensive. He was unwilling to risk a potential counterattack announced by the Byzantine emperor Manuel. Instead, Kilij Arslan conquered territory belonging to one of his Muslim neighbors, who then sought aid from Nur al-Din. When Kilij Arslan refused to abandon the cities of Malatya and Sivas, which he had captured, Nur al-Din attacked him, in the summer of 1173, and, after several military successes, quickly forced him to sue for peace. One of the conditions of the peace agreement reached between the two sides was that Kilij Arslan would provide evidence of his correct belief and promise to undertake a joint campaign with Nur al-Din against the Byzantines. Nur al-Din could not have established any more clearly his credentials as a champion of Islam. However, it must also be kept in mind that in the eyes of the very pious, Kilij Arslan could not have been a good Muslim, because his court included astrologers, whom Kilij Arslan and his successors treated with great respect. Also in the summer of 1173, Nur al-Din succeeded in obtaining a charter from the caliph in Baghdad that declared and recognized Nur al-Din's area of rule to include Syria and Egypt as well as northern Mesopotamia, Armenia, and southern Anatolia. Nur al-Din obtained this recognition from the caliph despite the fact that he did not have even indirect control over the sultanate of Konya. All of this shows that the conquest of the Islamic empire of the Rum-Seljuks was no less important to Nur al-Din than the conquest of the Christian Crusader states.

Nur al-Din's policy toward the Franks was confined, during the final years of his life, to smaller military actions. In September 1171, in the course of a two-pronged attack on the principality of Antioch and the county of Tripoli, he succeeded in capturing the city of 'Arqa. He could launch a major assault that might have wide-ranging importance only if he could be sure that he had the support of Saladin and the resources of Egypt. The two unsuccessful operations, noted above, that Nur al-Din undertook in April 1170 and October 1171 against the fortress of Karak, were intended less to further the struggle against the Franks than to secure the ties between Syria and Egypt. The rapid transmission of important information throughout Nur al-Din's extensive empire could not be achieved by horse or camel. Rather, shortly after the Fatimids had been deposed, Nur al-Din established a comprehensive system of carrier pigeon stations.

In addition, Nur al-Din did not shy away from receiving at his court Mleh, the younger brother of the Armenian king Thoros, who had died in December 1168. Nur al-Din provided Mleh with troops in Cilicia to help him to gain the throne and, in so doing, provided military support to a Christian. He did this, as he justified himself to several critics, as a means in his struggle against the Byzantines and the Franks.

In both theory and practice, Nur al-Din expended enormous effort to expand and defend the Sunni orthodox branch of Islam. He established a "house of justice" (Ar. *dar al-'adl*) as the highest court in Aleppo and Damascus. He took part personally in the legal proceedings. Every Tuesday and Thursday he heard testimony, in the company of the judges and the legal scholars, regarding the injustices people had suffered, in his attempt to correct abuses. As a consequence, among his other titles, he was called "al-Malik al-'Adil (the Just King) and "Munsif al-Mazlumin min az-Zalimin" (Protector of the Oppressed against the Oppressors). As a champion of orthodoxy, Nur al-Din increased considerably the number of theological law schools. The first of these was established by the Seljuks at the end of the eleventh century as an answer to the Isma'ili-Shi'ite mission and propaganda of the Fatimids. In addition, in 1170–1171 Nur al-Din established the institution of the "house of tradition" (Ar. *dar al-hadith*), to foster the study of the sayings of Muhammad as the basis of the Sunna. Accompanied by the most important emirs, he took part personally in the sessions.

William of Tyre was correct to describe Nur al-Din on the one hand as the greatest enemy of Christianity and on the other as a just ruler and a pious, God-fearing man. As a consequence of this duality, it is possible to conclude that the propagation of the jihad meant more to Nur al-Din than simply a means of satisfying his political ambitions, despite the fact that his policies certainly were inconsistent and demonstrated some contradictions. Nur al-Din was not universally mourned in his empire when he died in 1174. Indeed, when news of his demise reached Mosul, Nur al-Din's nephew Sayf al-Din commanded the population there to celebrate and to drink alcohol.

The Death of Amalric of Jerusalem

On 11 July 1174, barely two months after the death of Nur al-Din, King Amalric of Jerusalem also died. In his letter of condolence to Amalric's son, the still underage Baldwin IV, Saladin expressed his sadness about Amalric's death, his congratulations on the boy's gaining the throne, and his best wishes for the future. Among other passages, he wrote: "He should know that we have for him what we had for his father: an honorable friendship, a complete confidence, and an affection whose ties are tight in both life and in death." At first glance, this letter appears to be a remarkable expression of chivalry. However, in a separate letter to his nephew Farrukhshah, composed by al-Qadi al-Fadil, Saladin reported the death of Amalric and wished eternal damnation on the dead king, thus appearing to have been caught out as a hypocrite. His contradictory statements may, perhaps, be explained in the following manner. Behind the friendship with Amalric, which he stresses in such a striking manner in one case but does not otherwise mention, there may have been lurking a concrete agreement between the two men that is not mentioned in any other source. This interpretation is supported by Saladin's action in 1173 in the region around Karak. On this occasion, he campaigned against the Bedouins without, however, moving against the Franks despite the fact that Amalric at that time was engaged in the north against the Armenians and had left the border with Egypt in the south largely unprotected. The agreement reached between Saladin and Amalric may have been a defensive alliance against Nur al-Din. He was the only opponent against whom such an agreement could have been made. Presumably, Amalric assured Saladin of military support if Nur al-Din attempted to intervene militarily in Egypt. In return, Saladin may have promised not to support with Egyptian troops any attacks by Nur al-Din against Amalric. Saladin's policies toward the kingdom of Jerusalem in the period 1173–1174 seem hardly different from those pursued by the vizier Shawar.

Despite his agreement with Saladin against Nur al-Din, Amalric in 1174 planned an operation with the Normans of Sicily against Egypt. This campaign was intended to coincide with the rebellion by the Egyptian conspirators noted above. Amalric may have given up this plan when Saladin discovered the conspiracy in March 1174. In addition, the arrival of the Norman fleet at Alexandria may have been delayed. It is also possible that Amalric's plans were changed by Nur al-Din's death, in the aftermath of which Amalric attacked the city of Banyas, which he had lost to Nur al-Din in 1164. This campaign, however, quickly ended in a truce.

In considering the relationship in this period between policy and religious propaganda, it is striking that Saladin, who had attempted to extend his agreement with the kingdom of Jerusalem beyond Amalric's death, did not hesitate to use this truce to further his own effort to secure Nur al-Din's inheritance. Specifically, he charged the new ruler of Damascus, Ibn al-Muqaddam, who had purchased the truce with a money payment and the release of prisoners, with betraying Islam. In this manner, Saladin attempted to portray himself as a champion of Islam as well as a champion of the interests of the Zengid dynasty. The propagation of the jihad made it possible for Saladin to style himself as the true heir of Nur al-Din and to legitimize his claim to the power held by Zengi's successors, a claim that they justly perceived as a usurpation of their rights.

The year 1174 was undoubtedly decisive in Saladin's life. After warding off an attack against Alexandria by a powerful Norman fleet in a three-day battle in July, he successfully suppressed an uprising of Fatimid supporters in upper Egypt in August. He was then able to turn his energies toward the question of the succession to Nur al-Din's empire.

The Capture of Damascus

Nur al-Din's heir was his still-underage son al-Salih Isma'il. Several emirs were locked in a struggle to determine who would act as his regent. The eunuch Kumushtikin, who commanded the citadel of Mosul in Nur al-Din's name, succeeded in taking al-Salih with him in his flight to Aleppo. There, he threw into prison Nur al-Din's lieutenants and took over the government in the name of al-Salih. While Sayf al-Din hurried from Mosul in order to annex those portions of his uncle's empire that were located across the Euphrates River, Saladin recognized the overlordship of al-Salih and claimed that he would act as his defender. Several months later, having been asked by Ibn al-Muqaddam to intervene at Damascus, Saladin left his brother al-'Adil in charge in Cairo and marched with a small force of just seven hundred riders to Bostra, which he reached on 23 October 1174. He was joined by an increasing number of emirs, so that he was able to enter Damascus with virtually no resistance just five days later. He immediately abolished all taxes that contradicted Islamic law which had been reintroduced after Nur al-Din's death.

Saladin's effort, a short time later, to gain control in Aleppo failed, however, when Aleppo and Mosul bound themselves in an agreement with the kingdom of Jerusalem. Saladin was able to capture the cities of Hama, Hims, and Baalbek. He then defeated the armies of Aleppo and Mosul on 13 April 1175 near the horns of Hama. Aleppo, nevertheless, remained under the rule of al-Salih. The city later was forced to promise never again to join an alliance with the Franks and to support Saladin in his struggle against them. Shortly after this, in the regions controlled by

Saladin, Friday prayers declared him, and no longer al-Salih, to be the ruler. Also, Saladin's name appeared on the gold coins minted at Cairo. The caliph in Baghdad legitimized Saladin's usurpation of the power held by Zengi's successors. In response to a long letter in which Saladin listed all his merits, the caliph issued a charter in which he granted to Saladin power in Egypt, Yemen, and Syria, with the exception of Aleppo. Admittedly, the caliph did not grant Saladin's request to give him the rule over all of Nur al-Din's empire. In addition, the caliph commanded Saladin to defend the Egyptian coast against the Europeans and to reconquer Jerusalem, since all of the necessary steps to do so had already been taken.

Heading back to Damascus from northern Syria, Saladin nevertheless made a truce with Raymond III of Tripoli, the regent of the kingdom of Jerusalem, whose attack on Hims in January 1175 had forced Saladin to break off his siege of Aleppo. Although the truce with Raymond deprived the Zengid rulers in Aleppo and Mosul of an ally in Saladin's rear, they were still determined to carry on their struggle against the usurper. The result was another battle in the following year, on 23 April 1176, south of Aleppo at Tall al-Sultan. Again, Saladin was able to overcome the Zengids. As had been the case the year before, Saladin again treated his opponents very mildly following his victory, likely for political reasons. He made no effort to pursue the fleeing enemy troops, and those emirs who had been captured were released very quickly. He also used the occasion to spread his propaganda. In his words, he found the exceptionally luxurious camp of Sayf al-Din of Mosul "more like a tavern," thus providing his troops with an example of the type of immorality that ought to be avoided. Even during the campaign, Sayf al-Din could not deprive himself of wine, woman, song, or even his aviaries filled with doves, nightingales, and parrots.

Despite his success in battle and the mildness that he demonstrated, Saladin was not able to gain control over Aleppo in 1176 either. He was able to capture the fortresses of Buza'a, Mambij, and A'zaz to the east and north of the city. However, a renewed siege of Aleppo in July brought him hardly more than the renewal of the agreement reached in 1175, which now included the ruler of Mosul and his vassals in Hisn Kayfa and Mardin. Of the three fortresses that he captured, Saladin returned A'zaz to al-Salih.

During a siege of several weeks at A'zaz, Saladin was barely able to escape an assassination attempt in his tent by the sect of the Assassins, who had already made an attempt on his life in 1175. This group, which was allied with al-Salih, soon became feared in Europe as well for their assassination attempts. After a revenge attack by Saladin against Masyaf, the headquarters of the sect in Syria, the two sides appear to have reached an agreement, in August 1176. At the very least, after this point there were no further hostilities between Saladin and the leader of the Assassins, the legendary "old man of the mountain," as he is called in the Christian sources.

Just a few days later, at the beginning of September 1176, after he had returned to Damascus, Saladin married the widowed 'Ismat al-Din Khatun, the daughter of Unur, who had married Nur al-Din in 1147. She was not, however, the mother of Nur al-Din's son al-Salih. In this manner, Saladin stressed his legitimate role as the successor of the earlier ruler of Damascus. The death of this much older woman in 1186 appears to have affected Saladin deeply. A contemporary Latin poem accuses him of having become ruler as a false Joseph, by seducing her and marrying her after murdering Nur al-Din.

Campaigns against the Franks

After a two-year absence, Saladin returned to Egypt in September 1176. Besides the energetic rebuilding of the Egyptian fleet, he improved the fortifications of the coastal cities of Alexandria, Damietta, and Tinnis in order to prepare better for attacks from the sea. In the interior of Egypt, he seemed to be more interested in securing his rule against further pro-Fatimid revolts than against attacks from the outside. The former were particularly dangerous during the times of his absence. Therefore, he ordered that a wall be built to encircle Cairo and the undefended city of Fustat. Above Cairo, at the foot of the rocky Muqattam range that controlled the Nile valley, he also began to build a citadel of the type that was located in every important city in Syria. As the site for this citadel, he chose a cemetery that included several mosques. In addition to using stones from quarries located in the Muqattam range, large stone blocks were taken from some of the smaller pyramids at Giza. As was true in construction of fortifications in the Crusader states, the heavy labor was done largely by prisoners of war. The citadel was completed fifteen years after Saladin's death. The city wall remained uncompleted.

In the summer of 1177, a fleet from Norman Sicily plundered the port city of Tinnis. However, the presence of a Byzantine fleet in Acre at this time did not lead to a renewed Byzantine and Frankish campaign against Egypt. For his part, though, Saladin, in keeping with his propaganda, undertook a campaign against the kingdom of Jerusalem, in November 1177. Although he moved a considerable distance toward Jerusalem along the coast from the south, this campaign was less preparation for an attack on the holy city than it was a plundering expedition. It may also have been intended to divert the attention of the Frankish army in northern Syria, which had been reinforced by Count Philip of Flanders. However, it is also possible that Saladin simply hoped to exploit the absence of important elements of the Frankish forces. He had the prisoners he took during this expedition decapitated in short order. On 25 November 1177, he was surprised in the region of Ramla by Baldwin IV, who at first had retreated, with the last reserves of troops left to him, behind the walls of Ascalon. The numerically superior but carelessly dispersed forces that Saladin in great haste dispatched to fight suffered a severe defeat in this battle, in which the Franks also lost many men. His aura of invincibility was gone. Hindered by an unusual cold snap, days of rain, and pillaging Bedouins, Saladin was saved on his return to Egypt through the desert by al-Qadi al-Fadil, who had come to meet him.

Despite the defeat he had suffered, by the end of Ramadan, the month of fasting, Saladin was able to set out with fresh troops to Damascus in March 1178, arriving there in mid-April. Major military operations were well-nigh impossible in 1178 because of the drought conditions. However, in August a small Frankish force attacked the region around Hama. Saladin's lieutenant at Hama was able to ward off this attack, in the course of which many Christians were taken prisoner. They were sent to Saladin, who had them beheaded, one after another, by the men in his entourage. This action met the clear disapproval of his secretary 'Imad al-Din al-Isfahani, who turned his face away from the proceedings, and of his reliable advisor al-Qadi al-Fadil, who was not present at the time.

One year later, Saladin had his revenge against Baldwin. His nephew

Farrukhshah surprised and defeated the king during a plundering expedition against Damascus in April 1179. Another plundering expedition, by Saladin's troops in the region around Sidon, led on 10 June to a major battle at Marj 'Uyun, which Saladin won. Among the prisoners Saladin took were more than 270 knights, who were later set free in exchange for a large ransom and the release of Muslim prisoners. Odo of St. Amand, the grand master of the Templars, refused to be ransomed and died a short time later.

As a consequence of his victory at Marj 'Uyun, at the end of August, Saladin was able to capture by storm the newly built, and not yet complete, fortress of the Templars, located at the strategically important Jacob's Ford over the Jordan, north of the Sea of Galilee. After a portion of the wall was undermined and then made to collapse with fire, Saladin was no longer interested in accepting the garrison's surrender. From this point on, the knights of the order fought a desperate fight. The commander of the Templars preferred to jump into the flames rather than be taken prisoner. In vain, Saladin had protested the year before against the construction of the fortress, and had offered to pay 100,000 dinars to end the project. Now he razed it to the ground.

While one hundred Muslims wearing iron shackles were freed from captivity under the Christians, several hundred Christians were at Saladin's mercy. In accordance with Islamic law, he had the apostates, who had converted from Islam to Christianity, killed, as well as all of the archers. Beyond that, the majority of the Christian prisoners were massacred by the volunteers in Saladin's army, and the remainder were carried off to Damascus. The very deep wells of the fortress were filled with the corpses, and thus made unusable. Back in Damascus by mid-September, Saladin had his own losses to bear, since more than ten of his emirs, and presumably a much larger number of his lower-ranking soldiers, were suffering from an illness they had contracted at Jacob's Ford from the corpses, which had rotted quickly in the great heat.

In 1179, the Egyptian fleet, which had been rebuilt by Saladin over the preceding years into an independent unit with its own administration, also gained a success that demonstrated the increasing threat posed to the Crusader states by Saladin. This threat may well have made apprehensive the Genoese, Pisans, and Venetians, who had commanded the sea for several decades. In mid-October, shortly before the fall storms settled into the Mediterranean and made travel by sea almost impossible, Saladin's fleet made a nighttime attack on Acre, occupying the most important port in the Levant for two days and destroying numerous ships belonging to the utterly surprised Christians.

Lord of Aleppo and Mosul

The following year, 1180, Saladin was able to improve his position vis-à-vis Aleppo and Mosul. He won over to his side an important vassal of Mosul when he aided Nur al-Din Mahmud of Hisn Kayfa against his aggressive father-in-law Kilij Arslan II of Konya. The latter had, four years earlier, inflicted a crushing defeat on the Byzantines at Myriokephalon. However, he did not make use of this victory. Instead, he turned his attention eastward, where he attempted to expand his power at the expense of his Muslim neighbors. In response, he was defeated in battle by Saladin's nephew Taqi al-Din in 1179. Now, Kilij Arslan II demanded a return of the territories that he had granted as a dowry to his son-in-law, since the latter preferred a singing girl to Arslan's daughter as his principal wife. Aside from attempting to frighten the sultan of Konya with a blunt display of his military strength, Saladin also showered Nur al-Din of Hisn Kayfa and the latter's brother Abu Bakr of Mardin with gifts. In this way, he hoped to influence these two Artuqid emirs and other Zengid vassals and to win them over as allies.

At the end of June 1180, Sayf al-Din died in Mosul. Less than eighteen months later, at the beginning of December 1181, his nineteen-year-old cousin al-Salih was dead at Aleppo. The latter, as a pious Muslim, had refused to drink wine during his serious illness, despite being encouraged to do so by his physician. The unexpected death of the only son and heir of Nur al-Din was again a stroke of luck for Saladin, who now lost another opponent who might have caused him great difficulties in the future. Despite Sayf al-Din's intention, his successor at Mosul was not his own twelve-year-old son but rather his brother 'Izz al-Din Mas'ud, who also took over the rule of Aleppo without shedding any blood following the death of al-Salih. He married al-Salih's mother, and had the treasury carried back to Mosul. Saladin, who remained in Egypt in 1181, was not able to forestall these events, despite his orders to his nephews at Damascus and Hama to do so.

As a result of the unification of Aleppo and Mosul under Zengid rule, Saladin could not avoid another military conflict. He renewed his earlier allegation that the caliph al-Mustadi, who had died in 1180, had invested him with the government of Aleppo. In addition, he sent accusations to the new caliph, al-Nasir, that 'Izz al-Din of Mosul was maintaining friendly relations with the Franks and the Assassins. Saladin based these accusations on the numerous letters he had acquired, the most recent of which he sent as proof to the caliph. After spending 1181 reforming various elements of government administration in Cairo, Saladin left Egypt in May 1182, never to see it again. A surprise attack by his fleet and army against Beirut in August was unsuccessful. He then headed toward Aleppo, which he reached on 19 September. Saladin decided against a siege of the city, because during his march there, he had been asked by the governor of Harran, a vassal of Mosul, to cross the Euphrates and take over the rule of the territories on the other side of the river. In return, Saladin promised to allow all of the city governors that they could keep their positions if they joined his side and supported his war against the unbelievers. As a result, in October he was able to gain control of the territories east of the Euphrates that had been ruled by Nur al-Din and then had been annexed by Mosul following his death in 1174. He did so without any noteworthy resistance.

However, Saladin was not satisfied with this success. After his capture of Nisibin, he decided, again at the suggestion of the governor of Harran, to attack Mosul itself. Saladin sent to the caliph in Baghdad accusations that the ruler of Mosul had paid the Franks to undertake an attack against him. Indeed, there was a plundering expedition in southern Syria that resulted in their recapture of the fortress of Habis Jaldak. Saladin also accused the ruler of Mosul of oppressing his subjects and of asking for aid from the Seljuk sultan in Persia, the declared enemy of the caliph. This last accusation is substantiated by sources from Mosul. Since 'Izz al-Din of Mosul had attempted to gain the support of the caliph for himself against Saladin, the usurper of the Zengid inheritance, al-Nasir began to mediate between the two opponents.

Contrary to the expectations of Saladin and his advisors, 'Izz al-Din did not flee Mosul. Instead, he undertook an energetic defense. In addition,

Aleppo remained militarily active to Saladin's rear. After he had besieged Mosul for four weeks in vain, Saladin, in the company of the caliph's emissaries, headed west in the direction of Sinjar. He was able to break through the outer defenses, but did not gain entrance to the city itself. By the beginning of the fasting month of Ramadan, at the end of December, his efforts appeared to be flagging. The defenders, who had become inattentive as a result, and perhaps also having been betrayed, were not able to ward off a sudden assault. The defenders capitulated in January 1183 in return for their free departure from the city. The final victory was achieved without a major blood bath, which would have hurt Saladin's future efforts. In this manner, Saladin won an important base for the continuation of his campaign against Mosul. He hurried once more to confirm with the caliph that he was acting in accordance with the obligations he had been assigned as part of his charter of investiture, and to criticize Mosul for its putative alliance with the Franks. He also claimed that the troops from Mosul were required for his struggle against the Franks.

After his capture of Sinjar, Saladin decided to resume his operations in the following spring. He marched via Nisibin to Harran, and finally permitted his soldiers to depart for home late in February. In Nisibin, the citizens complained about the city governor. Saladin replaced him with another man in order to prevent displeasure at the governor's rule from increasing. In April 1183, Saladin set out for further conquests. An army, composed of troops drawn from Mosul, Aleppo, Mardin, Khilat, and Bitlis, which had assembled in the meantime, retreated before him, and then dispersed. Since the caliph had given him the title to Amid, rather than to Mosul, he attacked this fortress, which was located on the Tigris and considered virtually unconquerable, and captured it after a two-week siege. When it seemed clear that the fortress could be taken by storm, the commander, who was not beloved by the population, capitulated because he feared betrayal. Saladin permitted the commander to leave with his personal property. He then granted Amid with all of its provisions and weapons to the Artuqid Nur al-Din of Hisn Kayfa, who freed the population from all illegal taxes. This great military success induced the Artuqid emirs of Mardin and Mayyafariqin also to turn their backs on the Zengid cause and to join Saladin.

By no means did Saladin lose sight of his goal of capturing Mosul during this period. In his letters, he claimed that if the caliph had granted him the rule of the city, Mosul would have long since been in his hands. He also claimed that the possession of Mosul would permit him to conquer Jerusalem, Constantinople, Georgia, and the Maghreb.

At the same time, Saladin again led his army against Aleppo. On the march there, he captured the town of Tall Khalid, located west of the Euphrates, without a struggle. A short time later, he also captured 'Ayntab to the north. Approaching from the north, he appeared before Aleppo on 21 May 1183. As before, however, the population of the city refused to open the gates to him. There was a battle during which Nur al-Din's former bodyguard fought bravely for the Zengid cause. Nevertheless, 'Imad al-Din Zengi, the governor and brother of 'Izz al-Din of Mosul, preferred to come to terms with Saladin peacefully. Although Saladin at first hesitated to do so, he finally agreed to an exchange with Zengi on 11 June. The latter promised to support Saladin with troops for the struggle against the Franks. In return for not occupying Aleppo, he was to receive the city of Sinjar, which had previously belonged to him, as well as Khabur, Nisibin, Raqqa, and Saruj. The next day, to the surprise of the population, the yellow banners of Saladin flew above the citadel of Aleppo. Despite his continuous shortage of money, Saladin permitted Zengi to take with him all of the supplies and military equipment that he was able to carry and then purchased part of the remaining supplies from him. On 21 June, Sinjar and the other cities, noted above, were handed over to Zengi, and one day later Saladin marched into Aleppo. With the exception of the Crusader states, all of Syria was now under his rule. As he was accustomed to doing, Saladin abolished all of the illegal taxes in Aleppo. He treated Nur al-Din's erstwhile bodyguard with courtesy, which must have pleased them. He did not wish to do without the fighting strength of his earlier brothers-in-arms.

In the months following his capture of Aleppo, additional emirs in Mesopotamia joined Saladin. As a result, 'Izz al-Din of Mosul lost control not only over the city of Haditha on the Euphrates but also the two cities of Jazirat ibn 'Umar and Tikrit, which were located to the north and south of Mosul on the Tigris. He also lost Irbil to the east, which was located between the greater and lesser Zab. Without naming names, in July or August 1183, the caliph had already granted to Saladin those territories and cities that did not obey the commands of the caliph and were to be brought under Saladin's control. Saladin interpreted this command to suit his own purposes and, at the end of February 1184, decided to support the emirs of these cities against 'Izz al-Din. In spring 1184, the latter vainly attempted to gain back control of Irbil with the aid of Persian troops from Azerbayjan. The latter behaved extraordinarily badly by plundering and brutalizing the population in ways uncommon among Muslims.

Saladin's two attacks, in 1183 and 1184, against the strategically important fortress of Karak, which was an outpost of Frankish rule to the east of the Dead Sea, were unsuccessful. In spring 1185, therefore, he decided to agree to a truce with the kingdom of Jerusalem, an action that had been proposed by Raymond III of Tripoli. In this way, he secured his rear for a renewed attack on Mosul. In May 1185, he crossed the Euphrates with his army. Despite the menace directed against him by Kilij Arslan II, who sought to assemble a coalition of powers that were threatened by Saladin's undertaking, Saladin began soon after this to besiege Mosul. He increased the psychological pressure on the defenders by dividing up the military fiefs of Mosul among his own emirs. The summer heat began to get the better of Saladin's troops, and the possibility of diverting the course of the Tigris was discussed as a means of denying water supplies to Mosul. Before it came to this, however, Saladin decided to move northward in order to intervene in the struggle for succession in several cities. He was successful in his efforts, with the exception of Khilat, which he was not able to bring under his control.

In November 1185, he returned to the region of Mosul, but he did not undertake a regular siege. At the beginning of December, he developed a fever and grew very ill. He tried to keep this secret as long as possible. For this reason, he refused to travel in a litter when he broke camp on 25 December to travel back to Harran by way of Nisibin. He struggled for several weeks on the brink of death and only began to recover at the end of February. Shortly after this, on 4 March 1186, he came to an agreement with 'Izz al-Din of Mosul, who, even before Saladin's illness, had made clear that he was ready to come to discuss terms. 'Izz al-Din gave up to Saladin control of the turncoat cities Haditha, Jazirat ibn 'Umar, Tikrit, and Irbil. He recognized Saladin's overlordship of Mosul and obligated himself to supply troops for a campaign to conquer Jerusalem and Palestine. At this point, Saladin's power equaled that of his predecessor Nur al-Din, with the difference that Saladin could also be sure of his rule in Egypt. This is exceptionally important because the rigorously employed economic power of Egypt was to play a decisive role in achieving Saladin's military goals.

CHAPTER FIVE

Saladin's Triumph over the Franks

Propaganda and Causes of War

The agreement reached between Saladin and 'Izz al-Din meant that it would now become very difficult for Saladin to delay any further the major campaign against the kingdom of Jerusalem that had been the subject of so much of his propaganda effort. He could no longer attack his Muslim neighbors if he wished to retain his credibility. The pressure grew even among the ranks of his own supporters. Saladin's expansionist policies directed against Mosul brought the sultan into disagreement with his most important advisor, al-Qadi al-Fadil. The latter had, at first, expected a rapid victory. Then, bearing in mind the financial costs imposed on Egypt by Saladin's war, he argued for a peaceful settlement with Mosul, so that Saladin could finally attack the Crusader states.

Saladin took a long time to recover from his illness. Nevertheless, by the end of March 1186 he was able to travel from Harran to Aleppo. Then, on 23 May, he returned to Damascus. A short time later, al-Fadil demanded that Saladin swear in God's name that he would devote all of his attention to the war against the Crusader states as soon as he was physically able to do so. Obviously, al-Fadil saw the illness as a warning from God. This also seems to have been Saladin's view. At the very least, the illness made painfully clear to him the possibility that he could die before accomplishing his ambitious goals. In the following years, he frequently commented on the shortness of life and how much there remained to do.

This change in Saladin's personality may have been caused by more than his severe illness. He could also have been considering the death of his wife 'Ismat al-Din Khatun, which had been hidden from him until March because of his severe illness. In the weeks before he learned of her death, he had written letters to her every day in his own hand. It seems worthy of emphasis in this context that following his illness, Saladin now concerned himself with his succession. He no longer assigned all of the important posts to his brother al-'Adil and his nephew Taqi al-Din. He now had his growing sons take part as well.

Despite his triumph over Mosul, Saladin appears to have hesitated about preparing for a major campaign against the Franks. Aside from having agreed to a four-year truce with the kingdom of Jerusalem in 1185 (or to a one-year truce which was renewed for a further three years in 1186), the strength of the Crusader states while on the defensive was not to be underestimated. They possessed numerous fortresses that would be very difficult to capture as long as there was a Frankish relief army that could come to the rescue. This army, however, could not permit itself to be drawn into a decisive battle with the besiegers, but rather had to shadow the enemy forces, in order to hinder the attackers from storming the fortress walls. The goal was to create supply difficulties for the attackers and finally to drive them from the territory. As long as the defenders did not make any errors, this defensive strategy could only be overcome by the deployment of two armies operating in separate locations. Seen over the longer view, however, the Franks were faced with the question of how long they could permit their own economic resources to be plundered and wasted by the enemy without coming to battle, especially since Saladin renewed his attacks every year.

At the end of 1186, Reynald of Châtillon, the former prince of Antioch, violated the truce, and thus forced Saladin into an attack that was more than a mere plundering expedition. After Reynald attacked a Muslim caravan, which had to pass by Reynald's fortress of Karak on the route from Cairo to Damascus, Saladin demanded a complete reparation from the new king of Jerusalem, Guy of Lusignan. He only took up arms when his demands went unmet by the king, who was unable to deal with his vassal.

Reynald of Châtillon, who had previously demonstrated his greed for money as well as his lack of scruples, had for several years been named one of the worst enemies of Islam in Saladin's propaganda. This was because of his military actions in the Arabian peninsula and on the Red Sea. It was likely sometime during the winter of 1181–1182 when Reynald headed south in the direction of the oasis of Tayma', which lay along the eastern side of the pilgrimage route. He was forced to retreat by a counterattack launched by Farrukhshah, one of Saladin's nephews, against Reynald's barony in Transjordan.

From the Muslim perspective, Reynald's action could have been interpreted as an attack against Medina, or as a preparation for such an attack. In a letter to the caliph in Baghdad, directed against his Zengid rival, Saladin reported on these events, thus assuming the role of the defender of Muhammad's grave in Medina. He described the oasis of Tayma' as the foyer to Medina, although the two places were located more than three hundred kilometers from one another. It is, perhaps, on the basis of this letter alone that the historian Ibn al-Athir claimed that Reynald wanted to attack Medina. As early as 1174–1175, Saladin had described himself in a letter to the caliph as the protector of Mecca and Medina. He also had attempted to present his capture of the fortress of Ayla in the winter of 1170–1171 as a success in the struggle to protect the holy cities of Islam, because the grave of Muhammad allegedly was in danger so long as Ayla remained in the hands of the Franks. Nevertheless, Saladin's possession of the title "Servant of the Two Holy Cities" was first demonstrated in 1191–1192, during the defensive struggle against the Third Crusade, based on an inscription in Jerusalem produced at this time.

As Saladin had done in the winter of 1170–1171 during his capture of Ayla, at the end of 1182 or beginning of 1183, Reynald of Châtillon had several ships carried in pieces over land to the Red Sea. After they were put back together, the ships set course for the upper Egyptian port city of 'Aydhab in order to disrupt the sea lane between 'Aydhab and Jidda, or rather Egypt and Arabia, which was as important for North African pilgrims to Mecca as for the trade with India. Reynald's fleet captured about twenty ships, including one filled with pilgrims, and spread fear and terror on land as well, when they attacked a caravan heading from the Nile valley to 'Aydhab. After this, Reynald's force headed toward the Arabian coast. The Christians first attacked Rabigh, and then went further north to the port city of al-Hawra'. Saladin quickly mobilized a fleet that was able to catch Reynald's ships. The Franks lost the subsequent battle and tried to flee inland. After a five-day pursuit, the last of Reynald's men were trapped, and either cut down or taken prisoner. Two of the 170 Franks who survived were killed at the execution site at al-Mina near Mecca. The remainder were brought to Alexandria, and perhaps Baghdad as well, to be publicly tried and then probably crucified. Saladin issued orders that they were all to be killed, so that their recently acquired knowledge regarding the Red Sea could not be passed on. Reynald of Châtillon, who probably did not take part personally in this operation, did not fall into Saladin's hands. As a result of the Frankish plundering expedition, Saladin ordered that all non-Muslims be banned from the Red Sea, and thus from participating in the lucrative trade with India.

It seems likely that Reynald of Châtillon's primary intention in acting against Tayma' and the Red Sea was to demonstrate how far his power reached. In this way, he may have wanted to win back to the older routes the trade and pilgrim traffic that had been diverted toward the desert, so the Franks could again demand transit taxes. It is possible that his ships were headed home when they were defeated by Saladin's fleet. Their route indicates that they were not intending to make an attack on Mecca, and also makes it unlikely that they were planning an attack on Medina. The claim by the contemporary Arabic sources that the Franks wanted to conquer Mecca and Medina and then steal Muhammad's bones from his grave is, therefore, not trustworthy. Later sources even claimed that the Franks intended to take Muhammad's bones into their own territories in order to profit financially from the pilgrimages by Muslims to the Prophet's grave. Although this claim is not believable, it does seem to demonstrate the views of the Franks regarding Muslim pilgrims. However, it was not the Franks, but rather Arabian Bedouins, of various tribes, who frequently attacked caravans of pilgrims heading toward Mecca. Even Reynald of Châtillon, who was feared by the Muslims, did not attack pilgrim caravans. He was satisfied with attacks against Muslim trading caravans, as these were less well defended than the pilgrim caravans.

In response to Reynald's action on the Red Sea, Saladin attacked the kingdom of Jerusalem, but by the beginning of October 1183 the Franks still had not permitted themselves to be drawn into battle against him. He, therefore, returned in mid-October to Damascus, where he appeared to be settling the Ayyubid troops into their winter quarters, having ended military campaigning for the year. In fact, however, Saladin undertook an attack against the fortress of Karak at the end of November. With this fortress, Reynald of Châtillon controlled the one direct connection, at that time, between the Egyptian and Syrian parts of the Ayyubid empire. But Saladin failed in his attempt to surprise the enemy. The Muslims were able to capture the city but not the fortress itself. Since the fasting month of Ramadan was going to begin on 18 December, Saladin ordered a withdrawal. In his campaign in August 1184, he brought all of the materiel that would be required for a longer siege. Nevertheless, he again withdrew without success in the face of a Christian relief army.

The Victory at Hattin

The decisive battle came in the summer of 1187. By means of a cleverly planned and energetically executed attack on the city of Tiberias, located on the Sea of Galilee, the defenders soon after found themselves in a difficult position. Saladin was able to draw the Frankish relief army, plagued by major internal dissent, into a battle. The Christian troops, who suffered from a lack of water under the searing sun, tried in vain to reach the shore of the sea. In a two-day battle, on 3 and 4 July, between the numerically evenly matched armies, the Christians faced a devastating defeat, after the Muslims succeeded in separating the foot soldiers from the mounted troops. The victory and its aftermath could hardly have been a greater success for Saladin. Along with the vast majority of the Christian troops, he also took prisoner King Guy of Lusignan, Reynald of Châtillon, and Gerard of Rideford, the Templar grand master. In addition, the booty won by the Muslims included the relic of the Holy Cross that the Christians had brought to the battle. Several years later, this relic would prove to be an important pawn in the negotiations between Saladin and Richard Lionheart. After the end of the battle, Saladin had the prisoners paraded before him, and he called to account Reynald of Châtillon for the latter's violation of the truce. Because he had sworn to kill Reynald, Saladin cut him down personally. Two days later, to the delight of the volunteers in his army, Saladin ordered the massacre of all two hundred of the Templars and Hospitallers found among the prisoners, except the Templars' master.

Since the Franks had summoned the *arrière ban* to strengthen their army, and thus had mobilized all of the available reserves, the severe defeat meant that there were insufficient numbers of armed men to hold the Christian cities and fortresses. As a result, within a few months, Saladin was able to conquer the greater part of the kingdom of Jerusalem. He was able to facilitate his conquests by dividing his army and offering free departure to the inhabitants of the Christian cities and fortresses if they capitulated. This strategy was by no means motivated solely by generosity. Saladin intended that his opponents have no time to regroup after the battle. There were certainly cities and forts that were captured by storm. The defenders of these places were carried off into slavery, as was the case at Nazareth, Caesarea, Haifa, and Arsuf, among others.

By 5 July 1187, Saladin had succeeded in capturing the citadel of Tiberias, which had continued to hold out after the capture of the city. In this case, he offered the defenders the opportunity to depart freely. At the same time, one of his emirs captured the city of Nazareth by storm and made clear to the Frankish elements of the population what would happen if they did not immediately open the gate to the victors of Hattin. On Friday, 10 July, Saladin's troops were able to enter the port city of Acre, the actual center of the kingdom of Jerusalem. With assurances of protection for their lives and property, Saladin permitted the inhabitants either to depart from Acre or to submit to his rule and pay the customary Muslim head tax (Ar. *jizya*). However, not trusting his promises, the majority of the population fled by sea. As a consequence, the Ayyubid troops captured considerable booty. Much of the wealth of the city, which Saladin would later need when he fell into severe financial straits, was squandered in the process. The cathedral was immediately transformed into a mosque, and the Friday prayer was held there.

Saladin reaffirmed his intention to the caliph to attack Jerusalem promptly. However, from a strategic and economic perspective, the holy city was of only marginal value. It was much more important to make use of the breakthrough to the coast, achieved through the capture of Acre, to prevent the arrival by sea of Christian support from Europe. If Saladin were able to take the port cities, the hinterland would not be able to hold out for long, cut off from all sources of aid. In keeping with this strategic plan, the sultan issued his orders from Acre. The conquest of the coast north of the city was undertaken by Saladin's nephew Taqi al-Din. His campaign, however, came to a halt before the walls of Toron (Tibnin) and Tyre. At the same time, Saladin's brother al-'Adil marched into the kingdom of Jerusalem from the south with his Egyptian troops. Since al-'Adil had been ordered not to engage in lengthy sieges or to lose any time unnecessarily so long as the possibility existed of easier conquests, he succeeded in taking Jaffa, but not Gaza or Ascalon. Saladin sent a column of troops from Acre, who in a short time took Haifa, Caesarea, and Arsuf, and captured many prisoners.

In addition to these actions, Saladin ordered the Egyptian fleet to sail to Acre. When the fleet arrived, Saladin probably issued orders that the anticipated relief forces from Europe were to be held off near the islands in the eastern Mediterranean. Since, during the Middle Ages, ships generally traveled from coast to coast and from island to island, but only rarely dared to make the journey over open sea, this defensive scheme would serve to blockade all of the Frankish ports at the same time. Two columns of Saladin's troops operated inland. Following the battle of Hattin, one column moved south along the Jordan River to Jericho. The other marched along a parallel course between the Jordan and the coast in the direction of Nablus. After the capture of numerous cities and fortifications, such as Samaria, Nablus, Baysan, and Jericho, the two columns joined up in the region of Jerusalem.

Saladin, himself, set out from Acre on 16 July in order to support his nephew Taqi al-Din. His success continued unabated as, ten days later, the powerful fortress of Toron fell. After this, Saladin headed along the coast and easily captured Sarafand (Sarepta) as well as Sidon, which surrendered on 29 July. One day later, Saladin stood before Beirut, which only opened its gates to him after a week of hard fighting. By contrast, somewhat further north, Jubayl (Gibelet) surrendered at the same time without a struggle, after Hugh of Gibelet, who had been captured at Hattin, offered to give up the city in return for his freedom. Saladin then turned around and headed to Ascalon, bypassing Tyre. Ascalon had tremendous strategic importance because, in the past, it had offered both Muslims and Christians the opportunity to attack their opponents quite easily. The security of Egypt depended, in large part, on who ruled at Ascalon.

After his army linked up with the troops commanded by his brother al-'Adil, Saladin appeared before Ascalon on 23 August. The example of Hugh of Gibelet may have convinced Saladin to have King Guy, grand master of the Temple Gerard of Ridefort, and others taken from captivity in Damascus and brought to Ascalon. He hoped to have these men mediate the capitulation to himself of Ascalon, as well as all of the other cities and fortifications in the district. In the end, Guy's efforts to convince the citizens of Ascalon to surrender their city without a fight in return for his release only bore fruit when Saladin's miners succeeded in making the fortifications of the city susceptible to an assault by storm. When the defenders decided that they were compelled to negotiate, Saladin offered them the usual conditions, including the freedom to depart. He was thus able to enter the city on 5 September. Following the capitulation of Ascalon, the Templars offered to surrender Gaza, Toron des Chevaliers (an-Natrun), and Gibelin (Bait Jibril) in return for the release of Gerard of Ridefort. For an unknown reason, Saladin did not release the Templar grand master until the summer of the following year, at the same time that he released Guy of Lusignan.

The Capture of Jerusalem

Saladin did not begin his siege of Jerusalem, where many Christian inhabitants of other places had gone to seek refuge, until 20 September 1187. Apparently, surrender negotiations had taken place before this date. Since his first attacks were unsuccessful, he moved his camp five days later to the area around the northeast corner of the city. Here, the terrain was more suitable for the deployment of siege engines. In this manner, he was able to bring down the walls in the same place where the Crusaders had succeeded in entering the city in 1099. The Christians hastily tried to repair the damage to the walls, but it was clear to them that they would have to surrender sooner or later. Nevertheless, the negotiations were very difficult. As the inevitability of a siege of the holy city had become obvious to Saladin, he only promised to forswear revenge for the bloodbath perpetrated by the Crusaders in 1099, when the defenders threatened not only to kill all of their own women and children and to destroy all of the valuable property but also to wreck the Muslim holy sites and massacre the estimated 5,000 Muslims who were being held as prisoners in Jerusalem, in order to fight against Saladin's troops to the last man. In addition, according to the Arabic sources and in contrast to later legend, most but not all of the inhabitants of Jerusalem were able to pay the price demanded by Saladin to purchase their own freedom. It was only by the payment of a lump sum, which was gathered with great difficulty, that about 18,000 of the poorer people could be saved from slavery. The remaining 15,000–16,000, including approximately 7,000 men and 8,000 women and children, were taken as prisoners by Saladin. On the other hand, to the annoyance of many Muslims, Saladin did permit the patriarch of Jerusalem to purchase his own freedom and all of the church treasures through the payment of the normal ransom that was set for a single person. In this manner, Saladin hoped to avoid being accused of breaking his word. Following the example of the second caliph, 'Umar, he also refrained from destroying the Holy Sepulcher, because even without it the Christians would try to make pilgrimages to the site of Jesus' tomb.

The keys to the holy city were handed over to Saladin on 2 October, and the Christians began to purchase their freedom. Despite the corruption and dishonesty of the emirs whom he had entrusted with this task, about 100,000 dinars flowed into Saladin's treasury. As had been the case at Acre, if Saladin had paid closer attention, he might have been able to put aside even larger financial reserves for darker days. Those Franks who were able to purchase their freedom were led under guard to an encampment that was located only a bowshot's distance from Saladin, himself. From there, they were escorted to Alexandria, Tripoli, and Antioch. Some traveled even further north, to Armenia.

The Eastern Christians, on the other hand, largely remained behind in Jerusalem. They accepted the obligation, along with paying their ransoms, of paying the head tax (*jizya*), and thus kept all of their property. In particular, the Melkite Christians had little to complain about concerning the change of power in Jerusalem. Saladin granted them the guardianship of the Holy Sepulcher, which was carried out by four priests who were not subject to paying the head tax. By contrast, the Syrian Nestorians and the Armenians did lament the changes.

Saladin attempted to make good at least part of the loss in population caused by the departure of the Franks by permitting the return of the Jews.

As a result, to some of the Jews he seemed to be a second Cyrus, who had freed their people from the Babylonian captivity and allowed them to return to Jerusalem. Some also thought that he might be preparing the way for the Messiah.

With the exception of the Holy Sepulcher, Saladin transformed most of the churches into mosques. In particular, in the Dome of the Rock and the Aqsa Mosque, he ordered the removal of all of the inscriptions, altars, and images that recalled the period of Christian rule. In addition, he had the pulpit (Ar. *minbar*) that his predecessor, Nur al-Din, had commissioned for this occasion installed in the Aqsa Mosque. Saladin established a whole series of foundations, too. The Church of St. Anne was converted into a theological law school of the Shafiʿite tradition. The house of the patriarch was converted into a Sufi monastery.

Almost miraculously, the day of the capture of Jerusalem, Friday 27 Rajab (2 October) was the exact date of the nighttime journey to heaven that Muhammad is supposed to have made from the holy rock in Jerusalem. Reputedly, the year, month, and even day of the reconquest of Jerusalem had been predicted by numerous men. Saladin knew how to present his success in the correct light, and he organized extravagant celebrations. The climax of the celebrations took place during the Friday prayer in the Aqsa Mosque on 9 October. This was the hour in which Saladin was able to justify himself against all of the suspicions that he had simply used jihad to further his own power at the expense of his Muslim neighbors. His propaganda had long contested the right of Zengi's descendants to legitimize the rule of their dynasty by claiming a special role as leaders of the jihad. In keeping with the words that his secretary and biographer ʿImad al-Din placed in the sultan's mouth, God had reserved the completion of this task, that is the conquest of Jerusalem, for Saladin and the caliph al-Nasir. Saladin had his success announced in virtually every Muslim land. ʿImad al-Din is reported to have written seventy letters in one day. And Saladin received congratulations from almost every side. In addition, Muslim scholars and pilgrims streamed in from near and far to visit the holy sites in Jerusalem on their way to Mecca and Medina. Some Muslims saw in Saladin the Mahdi, the one expected at the end of time, who would conquer Constantinople, Rome, and the whole world and undertake the spread of right belief and justice in the course of his struggle against heretics and Christians.

However, many Muslim rulers appear to have viewed Saladin's success with a mixture of mistrust and envy. The 'Abbasid caliph in Baghdad did not conceal his true feelings and was angered that the sultan did not send news of his victory at Hattin with a high-ranking official. Al-Nasir did not even grant Saladin a new title of honor, but rather took offense that Saladin bore the title "al-Malik al-Nasir" (The Victory-Bringing King), which Saladin had held since entering office as the Fatimid vizier. The caliph wanted to reserve the epithet "al-Nasir" for his own person. Although Saladin offered to give up the title if the caliph would give him another in its place, the relationship with al-Nasir remained tense. Saladin was never able to overcome the caliph's suspicions regarding his expansionist policies. In February 1188, an incident that took place at 'Arafat during the Mecca pilgrimage was certainly on everyone's mind. A fight broke out between Ibn al-Muqaddam, the leader of the Syrian pilgrims and an old Saladin loyalist, and Tashtikin, the leader of the Iraqi pilgrims, because the former had planted Saladin's banner next to the banner of the caliph. Although Ibn al-Muqaddam had done everything in his power to avoid an armed confrontation, there was still a melee, during which he lost his life. The caliph sent his regrets to Saladin regarding Tashtikin's lack of prudence, but he left no doubt that the leadership of the pilgrimage to Mecca belonged to Tashtikin, and that those rights would continue.

Al-Nasir, as well as other Muslim rulers, remained passive in the face of Saladin's subsequent struggle against the Third Crusade. Saladin tried in vain to use the example of the pope's involvement on the side of the Crusaders to convince the caliph to take an active role. The caliph, who was engaged in his own plans for conquest, did not send any troops. Instead, in April 1190 he offered to make a loan to Saladin, an offer that Saladin did not accept. The caliph had requested support during his own siege of Tikrit at the end of 1189, an action that must be understood as demonstrating either his disregard of Saladin's difficulties or his misjudgment of the dangers that Saladin faced. Al-Nasir may well have thought that these were simply further examples of exaggerations perpetuated by the Ayyubid propaganda.

The Setback before Tyre

Saladin departed Jerusalem four weeks after conquering it and headed toward the port city of Tyre, which was almost surrounded by water. He had entrusted the siege of Tyre to his battle-tested nephew Taqi al-Din. Surrender talks had already begun when the landing of Marquis Conrad of Montferrat dashed the hopes of the Muslims for a rapid capture. Earlier, Conrad had mistakenly dropped anchor at Acre, and had been lucky to escape the new masters of the city. While Saladin took Beirut, Ascalon, and Jerusalem, a blockade of Tyre was put into effect. Saladin arrived at Tyre on 12 November. Nine days later, his favorite son, al-Zahir, arrived with fresh troops from Aleppo. At about the same time, and despite the beginning of the autumn storms, a part of the Ayyubid fleet also appeared outside the port. The besiegers soon began a series of energetic assaults. The defenders were able to repair a portion of one of the three city walls that had been damaged during an attack. The outcome of the battle at Tyre hung in the balance when, during the early morning hours of 30 December, Conrad of Montferrat succeeded in overwhelming the sleep-deprived crews of five Ayyubid ships and driving off the remainder. The other ships, with one exception, were driven aground by the Muslims and destroyed, so that they would not fall into Conrad's hands.

The Muslims' fierce assaults had captured the first city wall and placed the second in serious jeopardy but were ultimately unsuccessful, so Saladin broke off the siege of Tyre on 1 January 1188. The greater part of his troops, accustomed to rapid victories, refused to fight any longer. Saladin did not think he would be able to subsidize any further the financial burdens born by his emirs because of their long absences from home. Despite the enormous booty captured in 1187, his financial difficulties had become so severe that he would decide to undertake a monetary reform in which he gave up the gold standard and adopted a silver standard. As a result of Saladin's decisions, the individual contingents of soldiers returned home. Saladin remained in the theater of operations, wintering at Acre rather than heading back to Jerusalem.

In addition to the port city of Tyre, at the beginning of 1188, Saladin was still faced with the task of capturing the most powerful inland fortresses within the kingdom of Jerusalem. The example of the Hospitaller fortress of Belvoir (Kawkib) south of the Sea of Galilee on the Jordan River, whose defenders had wiped out the Ayyubid besieging force during a nighttime assault, made clear the difficulties that Saladin faced in attempting to take these places. At first he had placed the task of capturing these fortresses in the hands of individual emirs. He only took over direct control of the operations later, because he considered the campaign in the north to conquer the county of Tripoli and the principality of Antioch to be more important.

To prepare for this campaign, it was necessary first to analyze the situation. In part because of the weakness of his fleet, Saladin had to consider whether the fortifications at Acre should be rebuilt or whether the city should be destroyed in order to make it unusable in case of a Frankish reconquest. Although he recognized that counterattack, and perhaps renewed crusade, were possible he decided to establish even better defenses at Acre. In fact, he could hope to take Tyre only if he had a base for his fleet like Acre. In addition, it would have made sense to destroy the fortifications of Acre only if the walls of the other captured coastal cities were razed as well.

The Attack on Antioch

Saladin hoped to undertake a whole new series of conquests in 1188. After the middle of March, he had to concede that he did not have enough troops to attempt to storm the fortress at Belvoir. Therefore, he entrusted the direction of the ongoing siege to an emir in command of five hundred men, and he marched to Damascus, where he issued commands in all directions to have troops assemble for his planned campaign.

Saladin set out just five days after receiving word that the Franks were marching against Jubayl, and forced his opponents to give up their attack. Subsequently, he headed north and gathered the columns of troops then arriving at Hims. After a probing attack against Crac des Chevaliers, he convinced himself that the capture of this fortress would also require a long siege and time that he did not have.

In the meantime, a fleet from Norman Sicily entered Tripoli, and the

now-emboldened defenders launched a successful assault on the patrol-
ing Ayyubid troops. For Saladin, this meant that it would require more
than just a few days to carry out his plans to capture Tripoli. As a result, he
gave up all of his plans regarding Tripoli. This decision was made much
easier by the promise of the qadi of the port city of Jabala, located somewhat further north, to surrender Jabala and the surrounding fortresses as
soon as Saladin appeared with his troops.

While Saladin's brother al-ʿAdil made a display of setting up camp
outside of Toron, in order to keep the Franks at Tyre in check, the main
army arrived at Jabala, on 15 July, where the qadi immediately flew Saladin's yellow banners. Six days later, the sultan appeared outside Latakia.
Since the Muslim elements of the population were ready to capitulate, the
Franks there decided against a lengthy resistance in return for permission
to leave with their movable property, aside from war materiel and food
stuffs, and to go to Antioch. During these negotiations, the Sicilian fleet
appeared outside the harbor. Because of the rapid surrender of the city, the
Normans decided to punish the population, so they stopped one of the
ships carrying the departing Christian émigrés. As a result, many Christians decided to remain in Latakia and to pay a head tax to Saladin.

On 24 July, Saladin's army headed northward to Jisr al-Shughr on the
Orontes River, thereby opening his line of communication with Aleppo. A
direct assault against Antioch along the coast was impossible for both
strategic and logistical reasons. Saladin could not afford to leave additional Frankish fortresses in enemy hands in his rear, because they could
threaten his supply lines. Besides, it was far easier to supply his army on
the route from Hama along the Orontes valley. He succeeded in taking
without much effort the strong fortresses of Saône (Sahyun), Bakas-
Shughr, and Burzayh.

No later than 24 August, Saladin was able to launch an attack in the
immediate neighborhood of Antioch. The open route to Hama and the
connection to Aleppo gave him complete operational freedom of move-
ment. Saladin at first refrained from undertaking a direct assault on Antioch. Instead, he turned toward the Baylan pass, which was controlled by
the fortress of Bagras, and the valley of Nahr al-Aswad, which was protected by Darbasak. In this way, he secured his conquests in the north

against a possible invasion by a European Crusader army. The capitulation of Antioch, which had been isolated by these maneuvers, seemed to be only a matter of time. After a fourteen-day siege, the Ayyubid troops entered Darbasak on 16 September. In return for free passage to Antioch, the surrendering Templars had to leave all of their possessions to the Muslims, aside from the clothes that they were wearing. The next day, Saladin appeared before the fortress of Bagras, which was also defended by Templars. His engines could not reach the walls located on the heights, and again there were murmurings in his camp regarding the length of the campaign. Obviously because of their lack of information, the Templars missed an opportunity to use this unrest in Saladin's ranks to their own advantage. They offered to capitulate under the same conditions as those given Darbasak. Thus Bagras was captured by the attackers on 26 September.

In the meantime, Saladin had received an emissary from Bohemond III of Antioch who offered to conclude a truce. Bohemond promised, in return, to release his Muslim prisoners. Since the emirs were pressing for their troops to return home, Saladin accepted an eight-month truce. If no help from Europe arrived within this period, Antioch was to be surrendered to him.

Although Saladin dispersed the greater part of his troops, he and his core forces did not rest, despite the onset of Ramadan. Rather, he marched via Aleppo and Hama to Damascus, and then headed toward the Templars' fortress at Saphet (Safad), located north of the Sea of Galilee in the kingdom of Jerusalem. The siege up to this point had so depleted the defenders' supplies that the fortress was surrendered on 30 November by the Templars, who then departed to Tyre. A short time later, Saladin stood south of the Sea of Galilee before the fortress of Belvoir, ready at last to compel its capitulation. At the end of 1188, since the Hospitallers did not deign to answer Saladin's demand for their surrender, the Ayyubids again had to undertake heavy fighting, in order to convince the knights of the order that their continued resistance was useless. Saladin's assaults were made even more difficult by heavy downpours and storms. In addition, as had been the case at Bagras, the besiegers lacked drinking water. Finally, however, their miners were able to collapse a bastion and open a gap in the fortress wall for an assault. As a result, the Hospitallers left their fort on 5 January 1189 in return for the guarantee of free departure to Tyre. Shortly before, in October or November, the negotiations were concluded for the surrender of Karak to the Muslims in return for the release of Humphrey IV of Toron and the free departure of the garrison. In the period following, up to May 1189, Montréal and several other fortresses south of the Dead Sea also fell into Saladin's hands.

CHAPTER SIX

The Third Crusade

Preparations in Europe

The reaction of the Europeans to Saladin's successes could hardly have been stronger. The news of the defeat suffered at Hattin worsened the already poor health of Pope Urban III so much that he died. Even before word of the loss of Jerusalem reached Europe, Urban's promptly elected successor Gregory VIII issued a call, on 29 October 1187, for another renewed crusade. Saladin thus was forewarned. However, the vast size of this third and largest of all of the Crusades appears to have taken him by surprise. Almost all of the important powers in the Christian West took part. Apart from the three large armies under the leadership of the English, French, and German rulers, other powerful lords, including the archbishop of Pisa, the Landgraf of Thuringia, and the count of Flanders, led their own contingents to the Holy Land.

As early as in spring 1188, the Norman king, William II of Sicily, who, in contrast to most Christian rulers, had his own fleet, sent a small force of two hundred knights to the aid of the Crusader states. These were followed in the summer by an additional three hundred knights. In addition, William appears to have been planning, along with his father-in-law, King Henry II of England, and his brother-in-law Richard Lionheart, an attack on Egypt. However, Henry's early death, on 18 November 1189, hindered these plans. Moreover, William also died in 1189, and from that point on the Normans of Sicily no longer played a noteworthy role in the Crusade. William's death disrupted the balance of power in all of Europe. To Saladin's advantage, all of the powers taking part in the Crusade now paid more attention to the conflict over the succession to the throne in southern Italy and Sicily than they did to events in the Holy Land.

The kings of England and France had often made clear their intentions to undertake a crusade. However, out of fear that the other ruler was simply waiting for an opportunity to attack in the absence of his opponent, neither Louis VII of France nor his most powerful vassal Henry II of England wished to commit himself actually to setting out for the East. Indeed, in 1185 an embassy from the Crusader states had come in vain to their homelands, where both Philip II Augustus, the successor of Louis, and Henry II had refused to accept the keys to Jerusalem which were offered to them. The horrible news regarding events in 1187 appears to have changed their attitudes. On 21 January 1188, Philip and Henry took the cross. As a consequence, both England and France saw the imposition of a crusading tax, the so-called Saladin tithe. All those who did not participate in the Crusade, including both ecclesiastics and laypeople, were to pay a tenth of their income over the coming year. Henry II had the tax collected with the same ruthlessness that was typical of his handling of financial matters. The sums that were collected were enormous, and they caused a storm of protest. In France, the tax faced such massive opposition that Philip Augustus abolished the relevant ordinance after just one year as a "monstrosity."

All crusade plans retreated into the background in face of the renewal of hostilities between Philip and Henry in the summer of 1188. It was not until the summer of 1189, after the originally planned starting time of Easter had long since passed, that the two kings agreed that they would set out with their troops on a joint campaign on 4 March 1190. Even Henry's death on 6 July 1189 did not alter these plans, since his son and successor, Richard Lionheart, who was one of the first to swear the Crusader's oath, in November 1187, took up the obligations originally accepted by his father. Shortly after his arrival in England on 13 August 1189, he issued an order to the English ports to prepare and build ships for the planned crusade. In order to finance this undertaking, Richard successfully offered for sale everything that could be sold: offices, baronies, counties, shires, castles, cities, and estates, without distinction.

After the departure date of 4 March 1190 was pushed back to 1 April, and then to 24 June, the French king finally set sail from Genoa on

Genoese ships, and cast anchor with a part of the fleet at the port of Messina on 16 September. Another portion of the fleet sailed directly to Acre. Richard arrived at Messina in mid-September. The English fleet had sailed around the Iberian peninsula without the king. The fleet took on board Richard and the rest of the troops at Marseille. On 10 April 1191, Richard set sail for the Holy Land. Philip had raised anchor earlier and reached Acre on 20 April. In May, Richard conquered the strategically important island of Cyprus; he did not land at Acre until 8 June.

The first Germans took the cross on 1 December 1187 at the diet in Strassburg. Emperor Frederick Barbarossa, who had already taken part in the Second Crusade, together with his uncle, King Conrad III, followed their example at the end of March 1188. At the same time, he stipulated that the German crusading army would depart from Regensburg on 23 April of the following year. He also sent envoys at this time to the rulers whose lands his army would have to cross, in order to negotiate free passage and the availability of reliable sources of supply. The responses to the emperor's request from Hungary, Serbia, and Konya were positive. The Byzantines set conditions, because they feared that the Germans wished to conquer their empire. According to several Latin chronicles, Barbarossa also sent an embassy to Saladin in 1188, threatening him with war if he did not return the conquests he had made in the Holy Land. This report is, admittedly, considered doubtful. The Arabic sources do not record anything similar. In addition, the two Latin letters, that were supposed to have been exchanged between the two leaders, and which had a broad circulation in Europe, are seen today as clear forgeries.

The Crusaders from lower Germany took the sea route and departed before the emperor. In addition, Louis III of Thuringia and, eventually, Leopold V of Austria set out by ship for Palestine. Barbarossa's army moved off late from Regensburg, on 11 May 1189, heading downriver along the Danube. The army crossed the Byzantine border at the end of June. In this period, members of a forward detachment dispatched by Barbarossa were taken hostage by the suspicious Byzantines and not released until the second half of October. The party had been sent, at Byzantine request, to oversee the carrying out of the agreement made between the two sides. On 26 August, the Germans occupied the city of Philippolis, which had been abandoned by the population. However, by the beginning of October, the march was already six weeks behind the planned schedule. As a result, Barbarossa made clear to the Byzantine emissaries that it was no longer possible to make an immediate crossing over to Asia. He moved on to Adrianople, which he reached on 22 November, and decided this would be his winter camp. The Germans set out again in the beginning of March 1190. To the relief of the Byzantines, the last of the German troops arrived on Asian soil by the end of the month. They arrived at Konya two months later, but not without fighting. After briefly occupying the city, which was the capital of the Rum-Seljuks, the Germans left it behind. However, when Barbarossa died on 10 June, while crossing the Saleph River, the German Crusader army broke apart. Only a small German force arrived at Acre in October 1190, under the command of the emperor's son Frederick of Swabia.

Saladin's Search for Allies

In contrast to the Germans and the other peoples of Europe, the Byzantines did not take part in the Third Crusade. Since they had friendly relations with Saladin, the Byzantines were accused by the Western Christians of having an alliance directed against the Crusaders. In reality, however, the Byzantines and Saladin never did conclude an agreement. According to the Arabic sources, in the period from the beginning of 1188 to the middle of 1189 Saladin sent two missions to Constantinople. The first was sent to obtain permission for Islamic preaching in the Byzantine capital as a trade-off for granting the supervision of the Holy Sepulcher in Jerusalem to the Greek church. The second mission escorted the preacher and pulpit (Ar. *minbar*) to Constantinople. On the basis of a letter sent by Saladin at the beginning of 1189, which provides news from Constantinople regarding Crusade preparations in Europe, it is possible to conclude that there was a Byzantine embassy, which may have met with Saladin at the end of 1188. An additional mission came during August 1189 in the company of Saladin's envoy, who had accompanied the preacher and pulpit noted above to Constantinople. However, the Byzantine representative died before the completion of his mission.

These sources do not permit the conclusion that Saladin and the Byzantine emperor Isaac II Angelos established an alliance directed against the Third Crusade. Rather, it was the case, as al-Qadi al-Fadil explained regarding the Ayyubid view of the matter, that Isaac Angelos resisted the Crusaders, insofar that he did so, entirely in his own interest. Therefore, Saladin would not have made any concessions to Isaac even if the latter permitted the Muslims to believe that he was acting entirely in their interest. Saladin had a letter sent to the Byzantine emperor in which he only reported the death of the Byzantine emissary. Isaac Angelos demanded, in vain, that Saladin explain his intentions by sending an embassy that could discuss the current state of affairs. By this point, the German crusading army had already departed the East Roman empire.

As little as Saladin could hope for from an alliance with Christian Byzantium, he had just as little hope of gaining support from the Muslim side for the struggle against the Crusaders. By the middle of October 1189, he had already made clear to his emirs that he was going to have to depend on his own resources. Nevertheless, shortly after this he still called upon every Muslim ruler for help. He may have done so simply to be able to show later on that, in contrast to almost everyone else, he had not left any stone unturned in an effort to aid the jihad. In fact, he had very little success in these efforts. It was not only the behavior of Caliph al-Nasir, described above, which confirmed Saladin's pessimistic assessment. In Iraq and Persia, for example, the rulers were far more concerned with their own interests, and certainly the struggles and tensions of the past years, when Saladin began to reach out his hand to Mosul, were not yet forgotten.

In addition, Kilij Arslan in Konya proved to be unreliable, although he had promised Saladin that he would do everything that he could to ward off the German crusading army. Kilij Arslan had maintained friendly relations with Barbarossa since the 1170s, and thus promised the emperor free passage through his realm in 1188. He was kept from keeping his promise when his son Qutb al-Din imposed his will on him in Konya in the winter of 1189–1190. In an effort to expand his own power, Qutb al-Din had made an alliance with tribes of Turkmen. Although he had also promised free passage to Barbarossa, with the aid of the Turkmen, he attempted to destroy the German army. It is unclear if this marked an attempt to fulfill an agreement he had made with Saladin independently of his own father. However, after Kilij Arslan was able to smooth over matters with Barbarossa, following the capture of Konya by the Germans, and then opened up the way to Syria for the crusading army, both he and Qutb al-Din made their apologies to Saladin. In a complete reversal of the actual turn of events, Kilij Arslan wrote that he had been hindered in his resistance to Barbarossa by his own sons. Saladin appears not have put any store in these claims. His biographer Baha al-Din Ibn Shaddad wrote that Kilij Arslan never had any desire to hinder the Germans' progress.

Saladin also sought in vain for help against the Crusaders from the Almohad ruler Abu Yusuf Ya'qub al-Mansur from the far west of the Islamic world. He did so despite the fact that al-Mansur, like his predecessors, claimed the caliphal rank in competition with the 'Abbasids, and Saladin had frequently presented himself as a champion of both orthodoxy and of 'Abbasid interests. However, the Almohad caliph had a powerful fleet, which could have been of great value in defending against the Third Crusade. Saladin may even have hoped for an Almohad attack on Sicily. Such an attack may have seemed even more likely to succeed since the Muslim population living in Sicily under Christian rule rose in revolt following the death of William II. Somewhat earlier, these Sicilian Muslims had asked Saladin, himself, to conquer the island.

The Unsuccessful Defense of Acre

Saladin appears to have dreamed of carrying the jihad to Europe, in order to conquer Constantinople and Rome, following the destruction of the Crusader states. The goal of attacking Rome can be understood most clearly when it is taken into account that Saladin saw the papacy as the decisive power in tirelessly summoning Crusaders to the struggle against Muslims. In the course of 1189, however, Saladin saw himself increasingly driven onto the defensive militarily, with the result that he could not carry out his campaign of conquest in the north. Originally, he wanted to send his nephew Taqi al-Din against Tripoli in the spring of 1189, while he attacked Antioch at the end of the truce. Instead, expecting the Third Crusade, he concentrated almost entirely on defensive efforts. Taqi al-Din received an order to march toward Antioch in a purely defensive move to keep Bohemond III in check. Working with the same intention, Saladin massed troops: near Hims in order to prepare for the eventual Frankish action at Tripoli, near Tyre in order to observe Conrad of Montferrat and Guy of Lusignan, and in the coastal cities of Egypt to ward off an invasion that he expected the Normans of Sicily to launch. Keeping in mind the events of 1174, the danger of such an invasion must have seemed even more threatening to Saladin because he received word of renewed Fatimid intrigues in Egypt while he was engaged in the siege of Saphet. In view of the social tensions of the previous years, because of which al-Qadi al-Fadil had warned Saladin against further overtaxing the Egyptian resources, such intrigues could have found fertile ground. Apparently as a consequence of this report, Saladin removed from their posts and punished numerous officers of the Egyptian troops who were purported to have established ties with the Christians. Concerning those ordinary soldiers who were found guilty of such contacts he contented himself with expelling them from his army.

At the beginning of February 1189, Saladin spent several weeks at Acre working intensively to prepare the fortifications of the coastal cities. After waiting for the arrival of Egyptian troops to defend Acre, he set out for Damascus, where he arrived on 21 March. In the meantime, Guy of Lusignan, whom Saladin had released from captivity in the summer of 1188 under the condition that he never again take up arms, became active. The sultan may have hoped that there would soon be a struggle between Guy and Conrad of Montferrat, since Conrad did not recognize Guy as king. Guy headed, in vain, toward Tyre in order to obtain Conrad's support. He found himself compelled to turn toward Tripoli, where a large number of pilgrims and displaced native Christians gathered around him. At the end of April 1189, Guy again went to Tyre, but Conrad still refused to open the gates to him. Guy, therefore, established his camp outside the walls, where the Pisans joined him. Earlier, they had provided valuable assistance to Conrad in his defense of Tyre. Their decision to change sides was even worse for Conrad because a large Pisan fleet of fifty-two ships arrived at Tyre at the beginning of April under the leadership of Archbishop Ubald of Pisa. In addition, the Hospitallers also appear to have turned away from Conrad.

In the course of his search for a base of operations, Guy of Lusignan made two attempts on Sidon. Saladin was able to ward off these attacks without much difficulty. However, on 22 August, he received a report that

Guy was marching toward Acre. Saladin reacted by summoning all of his troops who were not otherwise engaged to come to the relief of Acre. Although the Christian besiegers were reinforced by newcomers from Europe, such as James of Avesnes and Louis III of Thuringia, everything pointed to a rapid success for Saladin. By mid-September, he had already succeeded in breaching the Christian lines and thus in bringing large quantities of food supplies and war materiel into Acre. However, his efforts to use this advantage to achieve a decisive victory were hindered by the lack of readiness for action among the emirs and the garrison at Acre.

In the beginning of October 1189, the Franks went on the offense and drove into Saladin's camp all the way up to the sultan's tent. However, the Ayyubid troops were able to regain their footing. Under the force of the Muslim counterattack, the Christians could barely hold their own camp. They would not have been able to maintain their position at all if Saladin had not been forced by the concerns of his emirs and the very nature of the iqta' system to allow large numbers of his troops to go home. In spite of a serious illness, the sultan waited several days to decide to withdraw his remaining troops to Jabal al-Kharruba, not least for fear of miasmas from the unburied dead, to await the arrival of his brother al-'Adil. He had ordered the latter and the Egyptian fleet to bring reinforcements, arms, and provisions. As Saladin had foreseen, the Christians used this opportunity again to enclose Acre on all sides. They did not renew the battle, but rather strengthened their encirclement of the city with strong fortifications. Their ranks also were reinforced by the arrival of more Crusaders. However, the stores of food in the Crusader camp began to grow dangerously depleted, since further supplies could not be brought across the Mediterranean because of the season.

Renewed heavy fighting at Acre did not break out until March 1190. Over the next three months, fresh Ayyubid troops came from Syria and Mesopotamia, and Saladin moved his camp ever closer to the Christians. He succeeded in burning three movable siege towers, which the Christians had built during the winter. He was also able to restore the partially filled-in trenches in front of the city walls, which were intended to hinder the approach of such movable siege towers. In addition, some Muslim ships from Egypt again broke the blockade being maintained by the Christian fleet when Saladin and the garrison of Acre launched a simultaneous attack on the Crusader camp. Saladin's ships in the port also joined the battle against the Christians. In this manner, Saladin assured the survival of the Ayyubid defenders of the city in the near term.

Then, however, came the news that the German Crusader army had not been hindered in its march by the Rum-Seljuks of Konya. As a result, Saladin had to decide whether he should march to meet the Germans, in order to bring them to battle at one of the numerous bottlenecks in the north. In view of the presence of the Crusader army before Acre, however, he decided not to leave the fate of the city in the hands of the garrison alone. Instead, he remained, personally, at Acre and directed the troops of those emirs, whose territories lay along the route of the Germans into the Holy Land, to watch and harass the German army. Thus, among others, his son al-Zahir was ordered there, as the ruler of Aleppo, while Saladin's nephew Taqi al-Din, the lord of Hama, took up position in the area around Latakia. In addition, Saladin had the fortifications at Tiberias, Jaffa, Arsuf, Caesarea, Sidon, and Jubayl razed.

During the tense wait for the arrival of the Germans, the Christians suffered a severe setback when they undertook an assault on Saladin's camp in an effort to take advantage of the absence of the emirs and troops. Soon thereafter, they also learned that their hope for help from a strong German crusading army had been misplaced. The sneering and triumphant cries of the Muslims that the German ruler was dead and his army almost completely disintegrated rang in their ears. A short time later, however, a ship carrying Henry of Champagne arrived and dampened the high spirits of the Muslims. A whole series of other Frenchmen and also Englishmen had arrived before him. Henry took over the command of the Crusaders, and in this manner the French party achieved the upper hand in camp. The arrival of Frederick of Swabia, Barbarossa's son, and the approximately one thousand men remaining to him did not change the situation. Conrad of Montferrat had hoped in vain to gain superiority over Guy of Lusignan with the support of the Germans.

The Crusaders again suffered supply difficulties as the beginning of the autumn storm season severed their connections with Europe. Discouraged by the Muslims' successful defense and pressed by hunger, many Christians went over to Saladin. It was only with the arrival of a supply fleet in February 1191, a very unusual event for this time of year, that conditions began to improve in the Christian camp.

By contrast, Saladin began in this period to face renewed difficulties in keeping enough troops in the field. He was able to overcome the ongoing disadvantage of the *iqta'* system, which made longer campaigns all but impossible, by regularly bringing in new contingents and releasing longer-serving units so that he could field a force that was comparable to the Crusaders' "standing" army. In this manner, Saladin hoped in 1190 to keep his troops in the field until winter and only send them home when the fighting was clearly over for the year. Nevertheless, he faced open mutiny in 1190 from the emir of Jazirat ibn 'Umar. As if this were not enough, Saladin was also forced during the fall of 1190 and the early part of 1191 to send, never to be seen again, two of his best generals along with their troops to settle a succession dispute in Mesopotamia.

Because the Christians sent their ships to Tyre or the Mediterranean islands and gave up their blockade of Acre during the winter, and because they were physically and psychologically at the end of their strength, Saladin decided in mid-February 1191 to use the sea route from Haifa to replace the similarly exhausted garrison of Acre with a new one and to bring large quantities of supplies into the city. The sultan also permitted the inhabitants of the city to depart if they wished to do so. He was not successful, however, in making up the numbers of the departing garrison and city population with volunteers. By the time the Christians renewed their blockade, the strength of the new garrison had reached barely a third of the old force.

During April and May 1191, the fighting at Acre resumed with growing intensity. Both Saladin and his opponents received fresh troops. Above all, Philip II arrived on 20 April and raised the spirits of the Christians. However, it was not until the arrival of Richard Lionheart on 8 June that the military situation changed decisively. Henceforth, Saladin was completely driven onto the defensive. By 12 July, the garrison at Acre had surrendered. All of the appeals and promises of aid by Saladin could do nothing to change the views of the worn-down and starving defenders. Admittedly, they did not know what fate was in store for them. When Saladin declared that he was not in a position to pay the ransom demanded by Richard within the prescribed time, the English king saw this as an effort to win time and to keep him from setting out to make further conquests. Without accepting Saladin's offer for a short-term settlement to be guaranteed by the exchange of hostages, Richard had the almost three thousand Muslim prisoners, with the exception of the more prominent men, massacred. This bloodbath cost Richard the best tool he had for demanding the return of the Holy Cross, which Saladin had carried off as booty from the battle of Hattin.

Following the action at Acre, no Muslims wished to defend any cities or fortresses against Richard Lionheart, out of fear of sharing the fate of the garrison at Acre. Nevertheless, the hope that Jerusalem, at least, would never fall into Christian hands, was enough to incite Saladin's troops to an ultimate effort. Saladin had the fortifications of all of the endangered cities and fortresses razed, and he concentrated almost entirely on the defense of Jerusalem. In this manner, he could again make clear his claim to be the protector of the holy sites of Islam. Probably, it is no accident that inscriptions of Saladin with such titles survive from this time at Jerusalem.

It is quite clear that the Muslim commitment to the jihad against the Franks was beginning to wane. Aside from the interest of the emirs in their own affairs, this waning of support for the jihad can also be seen in the declining numbers of volunteers in Saladin's army from 1190 onward. Despite the rhetoric and propaganda to the contrary, it was actually quite rare to mobilize the fighting spirit of such volunteers. Even the sultan, himself, often required encouragement from al-Qadi al-Fadil to avoid sinking into despair. At the same time, however, again and again Saladin was able to summon his energy to motivate his demoralized troops for battle, even when he was suffering from severe fevers.

On the other side, the confidence of the Christians quickly was dampened when Philip II Augustus began to focus exclusively on returning home following the death of Count Philip of Flanders in the camp outside Acre. Philip hoped to settle matters in Flanders in accordance with his own wishes. He was unmoved by the entreaties of numerous Crusaders, and thus set out for home on the sea route in early August. He did leave behind the greater part of his army. However, because of the limited financial support that he provided, Philip's troops would soon have to depend on Richard Lionheart's money.

The Truce with Richard Lionheart

The English king now assumed sole command over the Crusaders and headed south in the direction of the port city of Jaffa. Saladin had leveled its defenses in the summer of 1190 because Jaffa might provide a base for the expected Christian attack against Jerusalem. Saladin tried, in vain, to make use of the long-standing superiority in battle of Muslim troops over Christian forces that were on the march. Richard, however, succeeded in keeping his ranks closed and only responded with a counterattack if the Muslims had no opportunity to disperse in the face of a charge by the heavily armored Crusader knights and then attack these same troops in the rear. The main burden of the ongoing skirmishes fell on the foot soldiers. Part of them protected the flank that was exposed to Saladin and the rear of the three ranks of knights. The other part marched between the knights and the sea. The foot soldiers on this side, which also contained the baggage train, were not harassed by the enemy, and so they were able to gather new strength before changing positions with their comrades on the left flank, who were under regular assault by the Muslims.

The Crusaders' advance was supported by Richard's fleet. Its primary responsibility was to assure the supply of provisions without, however, taking over the transportation of all of the baggage and increasing the army's maneuverability. Contrary to Richard's expectations, the fleet dawdled and was responsible for the comparatively slow pace with which the army advanced.

Although the English longbowmen largely kept the Muslims at a distance, on 7 September at Arsuf Saladin was able to bring sufficient force to bear on Richard's rearguard that they were compelled to launch a counterattack. Because Richard deployed his whole force, he succeeded in transforming a dangerous situation into a sterling victory. Richard appears to have had an opportunity to capture Jerusalem following the battle at Arsuf, if he had not spent costly time rebuilding the fortifications of Jaffa. Saladin used the time to prepare the defense of Jerusalem. Although

Richard defeated the Ayyubid troops several times, his two efforts to attack Jerusalem, in January and June 1192, were unsuccessful. As a result, the two sides undertook negotiations. In this arena, Saladin demonstrated his superiority over the English king, who militarily was almost invincible. Despite considerable internal difficulties, Saladin declared that he was only prepared to accept an agreement that did not include giving up the lordship over Jerusalem. In contrast, Richard Lionheart missed an opportunity to use his two attacks on Jerusalem to improve his negotiating position. Rather, he only agreed to enter negotiations with Saladin after withdrawing his forces, and thus deprived himself of a better starting position. Besides, Richard spoke too frequently about the pressing need for him to return home and so made it easier for his opponent to wring important concessions by simply engaging in delaying tactics. In addition, before the murder of Conrad of Montferrat by two Assassins on 28 April 1192, Saladin for a time enjoyed the advantage of being able to play off the English king against Conrad. The rival of Guy of Lusignan, who was supported by Richard, Conrad hoped to gain the crown of the kingdom of Jerusalem.

The three-year-eight-month truce finally agreed to between Richard and Saladin on 2 September 1192 included Antioch and Tripoli, as well as the Assassins. Contrary to Richard's suggestions, Jerusalem was not made into a condominium but rather remained under the sole rule of Saladin. However, the latter promised free entry to Christian pilgrims and also permitted two Latin priests to serve in the Church of the Holy Sepulcher. The Holy Cross, which was desired by Richard as well as by the Byzantines and Georgians, remained in Saladin's hands. In addition, the sultan obtained possession of the port city of Ascalon, captured by Richard, which would be important to future Christian attacks on Egypt. Saladin subsequently ordered the demolition of the fortifications there that Richard had rebuilt. The agreement left the coastal strip between Acre and Jaffa, which the Crusaders had reconquered, in Christian hands. The cities of Lydda and Ramla, which were located inland, were to be ruled jointly by the Muslims and Christians as condominiums.

Richard Lionheart, who was very ill, was not able to set sail for home until 9 October 1192, shortly before the beginning of the fall storms. In contrast to many of his knights and Bishop Hubert of Salisbury, the latter being given the honor of speaking with Saladin, Richard did not take the opportunity to visit the holy sites in Jerusalem. Thus, just as the French king who had departed a year earlier, Richard did not fulfill his crusading vow. Aside from difficulties posed by his illness, Richard may, perhaps, also have wanted to make clear that he did not consider his crusade to be finished, and that he intended to return to the Holy Land with new troops.

Both sides saw the truce, which had been dictated by exhaustion, simply as a pause allowing them to gather new strength and later defeat the enemy decisively. Saladin soon thought about chastising those of his Muslim rivals who had stabbed him in the back during the Crusade. He especially desired to intervene in the succession conflict going on in the sultanate of Konya in order to gain control over the route through Anatolia, which might be taken by future Crusaders who did not come by ship. He feared that once he died his empire would collapse and that this would provide an enormous opportunity for his enemies from the West who had not yet been fully driven out.

First, however, Saladin prepared for a pilgrimage to Mecca, a journey that he never did undertake. He postponed the pilgrimage for a year because he apparently shared the view of al-Qadi al-Fadil, who had made two pilgrimages to Mecca, that a pilgrimage by the sultan at this time would be an inexcusable error. Since the participants in the Third Crusade had not yet departed, they could undertake a surprise attack in breach of the truce and perhaps even succeed in recapturing Jerusalem during Saladin's absence. Moreover, within the empire there were a large number of pressing matters that had to be resolved. The most important of these issues was the crisis facing many farmers in the region around Damascus because of oppression by their lords. The second crucial matter was the wretched state of Saladin's finances. Saladin was not permitted to follow the example of his father Ayyub and his uncle Shirkuh, who had undertaken the pilgrimage to Mecca as the leaders of the Syrian pilgrim caravan. In the contemporary view, missing the pilgrimage to Mecca was far outweighed by the struggle against the Crusaders. Moreover, even Saladin's simple intention of going on pilgrimage is remarkable enough. Over a period of several centuries, not a single 'Abbasid caliph or ruler of importance made the pilgrimage to Mecca, until the Mamluk sultan Baybars in 1269.

Saladin's Death

Saladin lived only half a year after reaching a truce with Richard Lionheart. The hard struggle against the Crusaders had worn down his strength. As early as the beginning of 1186 he had suffered a life-threatening illness, and during the course of the Third Crusade he was shaken several times by severe fevers. On the night of 20–21 February 1193 he again succumbed to a high fever. Contrary to the claims of some English historians, he did not die after overindulging in food and drink as had been the case with his uncle Shirkuh. Rather, his body suffered not inconsiderably from his decision, taken against the advice of his doctors, to make up two months of fasting that he had missed. On the fourth day of his illness, Saladin's doctors drained some of his blood, but his condition worsened even further. He first lost consciousness on the ninth day, and thereafter gained consciousness again for only brief periods. The merchants at Damascus began to remove their goods from the markets because they feared his death would lead to disorder and plundering. On the eleventh day, his doctors gave up hope for his recovery. In preparation for Saladin's death, his oldest son, al-Afdal, accepted the oaths of loyalty of the most important emirs then present in Damascus, in return for a variety of promises.

Saladin died on the morning of the twelfth day, on 4 March 1193. During his final hours, verses from the Qur'an were read out to him. He is reported to have smiled and then died after hearing the words of sura 9 verse 129 "there is no God other than He, In Him I trust." His corpse was washed by a Muslim law scholar and dressed in a shroud. After the midday prayer, he was placed in a casket, which was draped with a simple cloth, and carried out from the citadel of Damascus in order to be shown to the crying and mourning people. Following Islamic custom, he was buried the same day in the citadel. Not until December 1195 was Saladin laid in his final resting place, a mausoleum built for him near the great Umayyad mosque. The tomb of white marble, which awaits the modern visitor to the interior of the mausoleum, was built in 1903 and fits with the pompous tastes of the late Ottoman period, but it is not at all consistent with the wooden original decorated with rich carvings.

After Saladin's death, al-Afdal gave rich gifts to Caliph al-Nasir in Baghdad. These included the sword and golden helmet of the dead sultan, as well as the Holy Cross, a fragment of which is supposed to have arrived in Italy as early as 1192. Al-Afdal was not, however, the only heir of his father. Saladin had ordered that his empire be divided. His three oldest sons received Damascus, Cairo, and Aleppo. His brother al-'Adil received the remainder of various regions of the empire. In the following years, the Ayyubid empire threatened to break apart because of the ongoing struggles among Saladin's sons. However, at the turn of the thirteenth century, al-'Adil was able to tip the scales and obtain sole rule, and thus secure the continuation of the large empire until his death in 1218. After this, there were further succession struggles among al-'Adil's sons, but the Ayyubid empire continued on for three more decades.

During his reign, Saladin was celebrated as a second Joseph of Egypt. Comparisons between the story of Joseph, which is beloved by both Muslims and Christians and is told in detail not only in the Bible but also in the Qur'an, and Saladin's own story were apparently compelling. They are found frequently in Arabic poems and chronicles and sometimes in contemporary Christian sources as well. On an entirely emotional level, it was appropriate for Syrians and Egyptians to adopt for the sultan the image of Saladin as Joseph reborn. Over time, Saladin was not able to serve the Egyptians as Joseph had done, as a bringer of peace and provider for all. He did carry out a comprehensive reform of the internal organization of Egypt and gave a new stability to a land plagued up to that time by palace intrigues. However, his ongoing wars plundered Egypt's economic resources.

The result was that the Egyptians regarded both the Turks and the Kurds as barbarians and treated the period of Saladin's rule as simply another example of Turkish governance. Turks had never been loved in Arab lands. In addition, in the Egyptians' view, soldiers were nothing more than simple highway bandits. This image was quickly confirmed at the beginning of Saladin's rule by the numerous attacks by the "Turks" against the Egyptian population. The frequent plans to drive Saladin from power, and the revolts directed against him, were not primarily based upon ethnic reasons. Instead, the rebel adherents of the deposed Fatimids were mostly concerned about Shia Islam and regaining their lost offices and privileges. They could hardly count on the support of the majority of the Egyptian population, which had remained Sunni even under the Fatimid caliphate.

Presumably, Saladin's personal reputation among the Egyptians suffered from the fact that he liked their land only a little, although he loved the comparison with Joseph and owed so much to Egypt. Nevertheless, the Joseph of the Old Testament also had never felt at home on the banks of the Nile, and in his dying hours had the children of Israel swear to carry his bones with them when they left Egypt.

Although Saladin's wars were not in Egypt's interest, they were very beneficial for the unity of Syria, and they returned Damascus to its status as the capital of a large empire. This may have secured the sympathies of many Syrians for the sultan. He may also have earned their sympathies through his frequent expressions of love for their land. He was particularly loved in Damascus, as is made clear by the anecdotes about him that circulated there and were recorded by the Andalusian pilgrim to Mecca, Ibn Jubayr. Despite their possible fatigue with the war, Damascenes' sadness at his death appears to have far exceeded the normal level. Perhaps here, al-Qadi al-Fadil was not the only one who believed that after Saladin's death the hour of the Last Judgment was imminent.

Nevertheless, there was some criticism of Saladin among his emirs, particularly with regard to his widely known generosity, which caused considerable disruption in his finances. This criticism seems to be more than only an echo of the strife that broke out in his camp during the Third Crusade. Displeasure with Saladin's rule can also be seen in the report by al-Qadi al-Fadil, shortly before Saladin's death, regarding the bloody unrest among the farmers in the Damascus region who were suffering under high taxation, and the contemporary complaints from the population at Nablus about a variety of abuses.

CHAPTER SEVEN

Saladin and Posterity

The "Noble Heathen"

In large part, Saladin shaped the European image of the "noble heathen." Because of their experiences with him during the Third Crusade, his European contemporaries believed Saladin to be a perfect knight, and in the eyes of some, even a secret Christian. Over the course of the following centuries a number of claims were made about Saladin by Christians, including that as a young man he was dubbed a knight by a baron of the kingdom of Jerusalem, that he had a Christian mother, and that he died as a baptized Christian.

However, it was not until 1732 that a Latin translation was produced of the Arabic biography of Saladin by Baha' al-Din Ibn Shaddad, Saladin's contemporary and adherent. In 1758, François Louis Claude Marin published the first modern biography of Saladin, in Paris. This work was translated into German in 1761. Voltaire's "Essai sur les moeurs et l'esprit des nations," published in 1756, may have had a significant impact on the image of Saladin. For example, in Chapter 56 Voltaire praised Saladin's clemency during his capture of Jerusalem in 1187. Voltaire had contrasted this mildness with the bloody capture of the Holy City by the Crusaders in an earlier work about the Crusades that was translated by Lessing in 1751. Regarding the death of Saladin, Voltaire wrote: "It is said that he ordered in his will that the same type of alms were to be distributed to poor Muslims, Jews, and Christians. He wanted to show through this command that all men are brothers, and one should not ask, when helping them, what they believe but rather how they are suffering. Only few of our

Christian princes possess such generosity and few of the historians, of which Europe has no lack, have done him justice."

The image of the tolerant sultan was presented by Boccaccio, who showed Saladin permitting himself to be taught by an old Jew using the parable of the three identical rings to symbolize Judaism, Christianity, and Islam. This image gained further attention in Lessing's 1779 play "Nathan the Wise" in which Saladin appears as a precursor of the Enlightenment ideal of tolerance and is presented as a model for every Christian.

On the other hand, Schiller's skepticism did not have much influence. Apparently basing his work on the Latin translation that was published in 1732, Schiller translated Baha' al-Din Ibn Shaddad's biography of Saladin into German, and published it in his "Historische Memoires" (Jena, 1790). In his opening remarks, Schiller raised the suspicion that Ibn Shaddad had concentrated on Saladin's struggle against the Crusaders to avoid discussing less honorable matters.

Several decades after the Enlightenment, the Romantics seized upon the image of Saladin, particularly through the works of the Scottish poet, Walter Scott. In his novel *The Talisman* Scott drew a very sympathetic image of the sultan and, as had been true of Lessing, permitted himself all kinds of license. Thus, for example, he presented Saladin entering the Crusader camp dressed as a physician and healing Richard Lionheart from a severe illness, although the two men never actually met each other face to face.

After sifting through and editing what is for the high medieval period an extraordinarily large and rich corpus of sources dealing with Saladin, modern scholars, beginning with Stanley Lane-Poole in 1898, have begun to provide an ever more sober assessment of the idealized image.

The basis for the European image of Saladin as a "noble heathen," despite the fact that the oldest Latin authors were not very flattering toward him, is Saladin's largely bloodless capture of Jerusalem. The loss of the Holy City drew the attention of the entire West to Saladin, and, as a result, many Christian historians wrote about his course of action. This manner of conducting himself was confirmed for Europeans immediately after Saladin concluded a truce with Richard in 1192, when the sultan refused the demands of his people to take vengeance on the Crusaders making pilgrimages to Jerusalem on behalf of the three thousand Muslims who had fallen into Richard's custody following the reconquest of Acre in 1191. In the memory of the Europeans remained a man, who was equally chivalrous in victory and defeat, who was able to curb the desire for revenge, and who kept his word without question.

It was by no means obvious, from the Christian point of view, that it was necessary to keep agreements that were made with those of another faith, that is with "non-believers." A Christian who wished to break an agreement that he had made with a Muslim could usually find without much difficulty a representative of the church who would declare, on the basis of ecclesiastical authority and the power of the priest to loose and bind, that the agreement was invalid. As a result, it is hardly surprising that the Muslims thought of the Crusaders as susceptible to breaking their word. A particularly clear example of this is the case of Guy of Lusignan, the king of Jerusalem who fell captive to Saladin in 1187. As a result of Guy's promise, under oath, never again to raise arms against the sultan, he was set free in 1188. Shortly after this, however, he was freed from his oath on flimsy grounds by his ecclesiastical supporters. It is also striking, in this context, that following the capitulation of Acre in 1191 and during his negotiations with Richard Lionhart regarding the exchange of prisoners, Saladin believed that he could only trust the oath of the Templars. However, the Templars rejected such an oath, allegedly because they themselves distrusted the leaders of the crusading army.

However, Saladin did not owe his image in Europe as the "noble heathen" and a man superior to most of the Christian rulers of the Middle Ages simply to his treatment of surrendering Christians and his demonstrated adherence to the agreements he made. Saladin's positive qualities also included his almost extravagant generosity, which impressed Muslims and Christians alike. This generosity played a major role in gilding his memory. Even Archbishop William of Tyre, a contemporary who did not view Saladin as favorably as he had Nur al-Din because he looked upon Saladin as a usurper of Nur al-Din's inheritance and as a tyrant ruled by arrogance and the desire for fame, characterized Saladin as exceptionally generous, in contrast to Nur al-Din, and also as a man of keen intellect. Perhaps William saw in Saladin a characteristic of his entire family, because he attributed this same generosity to Saladin's uncle Shirkuh. The archbishop was hardly the exception among his coreligionists.

While encouraging Philip of Swabia, the king of Germany (d. 1208) to be generous, the minstrel singer Walther von der Vogelweide praised Saladin's "milte," that is, concern for the care and needs of others. In the following decades, two other poets developed Walther's praise of Saladin. The first was Brother Wernher, and the second was Seifried Helbling, who wrote around the end of the thirteenth century. Even Dante praised Saladin's generosity. This image, however, hardly exhausted the European praise for Saladin. Around the middle of the fifteenth century, even a papal secretary, Flavio Biondo, in his "Historiarum ab inclinatione Romanorum imperii decades tres," described Saladin rather than a Christian king as the most excellent and learned ruler of that time.

Like the Christians, the Muslims stressed from the beginning Saladin's incomparable generosity in financial matters. It recalled the type of generosity that Muslims hoped for from the Mahdi, a figure who sometimes was thought to have a role like that of Jesus at the end of time. The Mahdi was expected to lead the Muslims back toward true Islam and to fill the world, ruled up to this point by injustice, with justice. He was also to demonstrate the highest degree of generosity and to distribute so much money that no one would take any more. Saladin apparently loved to offer gifts without having been asked for them. Saladin is supposed to have said that a petitioner who received all of the money from his treasury would receive no further benefit if he blushed in embarrassment at Saladin's generosity. Saladin's dealings with the Christians in 1187 certainly were not the first demonstration of his generosity. Rather, he had proven his generosity toward his Muslim opponents and allies long before, for example, during the capture of A'zaz (1176), as well as the capture of Amid and Aleppo (1183). Saladin also demonstrated exceptional generosity in less spectacular cases. However, he frequently was criticized, for example, after the capture of Acre and Jerusalem and not least following his death, because, as is pointed out in Lessing's "Nathan," his coffers were always empty. He at all times needed money, with the result that he was forced to introduce a monetary reform in 1187. Admittedly, Saladin did not show his usual generosity toward the French king Philip II. During the siege of Acre, Philip's white hunting falcon, which had no equal, flew off to find others of its kind. Saladin did not return the bird, despite being offered

1,000 dinars by Philip, because hunting falcons from northern Europe were highly sought after in the East.

His generosity was, in part, the result of political calculation. However, Saladin was generous not only to his defeated enemies and opponents, whom he tried to win over to his side. This behavior appears to have corresponded to his temper and his upbringing. Since he apparently could recite the "Hamasa" of Abu Tammam, an anthology of pre- and early-Islamic poetry, he may have adopted the ideal of generosity of the lionized Arabic Bedouin society that is presented there. Other of Saladin's family members, including his uncle Shirkuh and his older brother Turanshah, who died in 1180 and left behind very high debts for Saladin to repay, were famed for their generous gifts of money. Saladin was no spendthrift compared to Turanshah, whose behavior even Saladin criticized, although al-Qadi al-Fadil defended it because of its political value. Obviously, Saladin tried to reconcile his office as ruler with the ideal of true poverty, an effort in which the example of his predecessor Nur al-Din may have played a role. In his later years, Saladin did live an ascetic life and drank no alcohol. He wore simple clothing of linen, cotton, and wool, and shied away from unnecessary luxuries. It is notable in this regard that he did not build a palace. It was certainly more than a simple matter of propaganda when, following his second victory over the combined forces of Aleppo and Mosul, Saladin drew his troops' attention to the all too luxurious camp of Sayf al-Din of Mosul as an example of immorality, in an effort to deter similar displays among his own men.

The appreciation of Saladin as a chivalrous knight was hardly the only reason for the positive image of him among Western Christians. Another important factor was the very dark image of Islam among the Europeans; Saladin appeared in a particularly good light against this background. The Western image of Islam was marked decisively by the view that the basis of Islam was ruthless force paired with extreme cruelty. This was seen to be in stark contrast with Christianity as a religion of love. To the extent that Pope Urban II propagated the First Crusade as a response to the putative persecution of Eastern Christians by the Muslims, this negative image of Islam was effective in Western politics. In the West, people did not know and did not want to know that Islamic rule called for the sub-

jugation of all mankind, but not for their religious conversion. The inconsistencies in the Qur'an were sharply criticized, but it was not known that
these inconsistencies meant that Islamic rulers could, in practice, follow
different paths. Europeans did know the clause in the Qur'an (sura 2.256)
that there is no compulsion in religion. However, without being aware of
actual practice, Europeans considered contrary passages in the Qur'an to
be decisive. In this context it should be noted that despite corresponding
decisions in canon law, the prohibition on compulsion in religion was not
always kept on the Christian side either. In contrast to Islam, conversions
that took place under compulsion could not be reversed, because of the
sacrament of baptism.

The image of the "noble heathen" that was based so heavily on Saladin
had no effect on the negative impression of Islam among Christian theologians. Certainly, Saladin was an exception among Islamic rulers. However, people did not know or did not wish to know that his behavior was in
accordance with the commands and prohibitions of the Qur'an, so Islam
could not be such a completely reprehensible religion as was thought.
Moreover, he was not the only exception. His nephew al-Kamil and several
of the sultans of the Rum-Seljuks of Konya, whose names were also
known in Europe, came perhaps even closer to the ideal of the "noble
heathen." Instead of calling into question the negative image of Islam,
and perhaps as a consequence their own theological position, Christians
claimed that Muslim rulers who did not correspond to the cliché of the
violent ruler could be identified as adherents of the Western chivalric ideal
or even as secret Christians. Even during the Enlightenment, the image of
Islam remained generally negative because the level of religious fanati-
cism that had already been criticized in the Christian church appeared to
be heightened even further in Islam. The depiction of Saladin as an en-
lightened ruler did not change this situation at all. In considering the
question of religious tolerance, Saladin was seen again as an exception.

The Tolerant Sultan

A reading of the contemporary sources with regard to the question of
Saladin's religious convictions and his policies toward the Christians
makes clear that he was not a free spirit with philosophical interests but

rather a pious Muslim who observed the tolerance toward Jews and Christians required by the Qur'an. In contrast, for example, to the Rum-Seljuks in Konya, he was also not a friend of astrology. At the decisive moments in his life, Saladin did not put his faith in stargazers but rather prayed to God to provide him with inspiration. Such prayers, which also were disapproved of by strict believers, were often said at night in the hope that inspiration would come in a dream. His great successes may have led him to believe that he was chosen by God to carry out special tasks. He is reported to have claimed in 1188 that he was given by God the task of setting the world in order. In 1192 he reportedly described his struggle against the Crusaders as a task that was given to him by God.

Nevertheless, Saladin did not seek an unrestrained attack against the Crusader states any more than his predecessor Nur al-Din had done. Instead, again and again he agreed to truces with the Christians so he could pursue war against his Muslim neighbors. The fundamental theme of his propaganda was the goal of the reconquest of Jerusalem. In fact, however, in order to destroy the Crusader states, which were very strong on the defensive, he needed to assemble an exceptionally large force that could be kept in the field over a period of many months through the regular rotation of the individual units. In addition, to undertake a major offensive against the kingdom of Jerusalem, it was necessary to have quiet in his rear in Mesopotamia. His ultimate goal does not appear to have been the reconquest of Jerusalem but rather the reestablishment of the Islamic empire under his own rule.

Although Saladin ended the Isma'ili-Shi'ite Fatimid caliphate in Cairo in 1171 and thereafter attempted to assume a role as champion of Sunni Islam, that is Islamic orthodoxy, Shi'ites who lived under his rule were not persecuted. There can be no question that, in contrast to the period of Nur al-Din's rule, the Shi'ites in Aleppo and the rest of northern Syria enjoyed a period of peace under Saladin, and even supported him. By contrast, Nur al-Din's propaganda had set the Shi'ites at the same level as the Franks of the Crusader states. However, Saladin did follow Nur al-Din's example of building theological law schools for the defense and expansion of Sunni Islam.

Saladin, like Nur al-Din, demonstrated his positive view of Islamic mystics (Ar. sing. *sufi*) by establishing endowments for them. They could also be found as volunteers in his army. His sympathy for mystical currents did have its limits, as was made clear by the case of al-Suhrawardi, one of the greatest Islamic mystics, who was accused of heresy at Aleppo in 1191. Even Saladin's favorite son, al-Zahir, could not save him from the death penalty demanded by Islamic law for apostasy.

Not only Muslim physicians, but Jewish and Christian doctors as well enjoyed Saladin's trust. This should not be seen as an unusual demonstration of tolerance by a Muslim ruler, since we also see Christian doctors in the service of the 'Abbasid caliph al-Nasir in Baghdad. This case is particularly striking because al-Nasir had ordered that Christians could no longer be employed in his state chancery. This led the majority of the Christian officeholders to convert to Islam. Egyptian Christians and Jews enjoyed greater freedom under the rule of the Fatimids than they did under Saladin. After the Frankish plundering expedition on the Red Sea in 1183, Saladin forbade non-Muslims from participating in trade on the Red Sea and thereby prevented them from participating in the lucrative trade with India. As a result, there ceased to be important Christian, that is Coptic, merchants in Egypt after Saladin's reign. Many of them appear to have converted to Islam. Nevertheless, even during the Third Crusade, Copts remained as irreplaceable specialists in important positions, particularly in the financial administration. Concerns that they intended to cooperate with the Crusaders turn out to have been unjustified.

Even in face of the threat of the Third Crusade, there were no persecutions of Christians in the lands Saladin ruled. Saladin dealt with the danger of cooperation between the Crusaders and the Eastern Christians in another manner. Following the capture of Jerusalem in 1187, Saladin succeeded in winning the hearts of the Jews and Eastern Christians in the territories that had once belonged to the Crusader states. The Jews were permitted to settle in Jerusalem again, which had been prohibited during the period of Frankish rule; and the Eastern Christians, in contrast to the Catholic Crusaders and their descendants, were never treated as a defeated people. Instead, they enjoyed the status of their coreligionists within Saladin's empire. Since they had not been treated equally by the Catholics in the Crusader states, they did not resist Saladin's rule at all. The Eastern Christians only began to suffer under increasingly difficult circumstances during the rule of the Mamluks from the second half of the thirteenth century.

Saladin had some of the Franks he captured in battle executed. According to Islamic law, whoever raised arms against Islam forfeited his life, and could be sold as a slave or exchanged for Muslim prisoners being held by the Christians. As it happened, Saladin at first spared the lives of the prisoners of war he took during the Third Crusade. When the English king ordered the execution of the roughly three thousand Muslim prisoners who were captured following the capitulation of Acre in the summer of 1191, Saladin did not give the order to repay like with like. He did, it is true, sacrifice some of his Crusader prisoners to the thirst for vengeance among his men. However, it is clear that the majority of his prisoners were kept as a trump card in expectation of future negotiations. He is also reported to have forbidden his younger sons to fall upon the Christian prisoners with their swords. He did not want the boys, who could not even tell the difference between a Muslim and a Christian, to become accustomed at such a young age to the shedding of blood.

Contrary to the claim of his biographer Baha' al-Din Ibn Shaddad, Saladin did not intend to wipe out all Christians, as Ibn Shaddad's own account makes clear. Instead, he undertook a friendly correspondence with Pope Alexander III and Lucius III to negotiate for the exchange of prisoners of war, a fact that is not recorded in the Arabic sources. It was straightforward propaganda when the historian Abu Shama claimed that following the battle of Hattin in 1187 Saladin planned on executing all of the prisoners but refrained because his troops did not wish to give up the chance of enslaving the prisoners and reaping the potential profits.

When considering Saladin's relationship with the knights of the military orders, the champions of the Christians, it should be noted that following the battle of Hattin he had all of the two hundred Templars and Hospitallers who had been taken captive massacred, with the sole exception of the grand master of the Templars. In doing so, he received the praise of the volunteers in his army. Saladin's action was intended, apparently, to rid the world of both orders. A corresponding command was sent to Damascus where the (presumably fewer) Templars and Hospitallers being held there were executed, too. An exception was made for those who accepted the offer to convert to Islam. In previous years, however, Saladin had not executed all of the Templars whom he captured. In 1184, a son of his nephew Taqi al-Din was released after more than seven years in Christian captivity in return for a large ransom and all of the Templars whom Saladin then held. Saladin also did not wage war against the Templars and Hospitallers in a blind rage. These knights even enjoyed a certain esteem. In 1187, Saladin permitted ten Hospitallers to remain for one year in the Holy City to care for the sick. Furthermore, in 1191, as noted above, the only Christians whose oath Saladin was prepared to trust were the Templars.

Saladin's behavior showed that he did not intend to force Christians to convert to Islam, just as the conduct of the jihad by Muslims was also, apparently, never intended to be a war of proselytization. In this context, it is crucial to consider what Joinville had to say in his eyewitness account of the crusade launched to conquer Egypt in the mid-thirteenth century by Saint Louis, the king of France. According to Joinville's account, the French who were captured by the Muslims were given the choice of either converting to Islam or being beheaded. Joinville protested this demand by referring to Saladin, as the following passage makes clear:

> While the other sick men were carried off to the galleys, where they lay as captives, the Saracens stood ready with drawn swords and killed all those who fell down, and then tossed them into the water. I said to these butchers through my Saracen interpreter that this was unjust since it went against one of Saladin's commands that prohibited the killing of any man after he had been offered bread and salt to eat. But they answered that these men were of no use since they could not even stay on their feet because of their illness. The admiral had my shipmates brought before me, and said to me that they had all denied their faith. I told him that he should not depend on them since they would leave the service of another man as quickly as they had left our service, as soon as the time and place seemed propitious to do so. The admiral answered me saying that he agreed. Saladin had said that it had never happened that a bad Christian was transformed into a good Muslim, and that a bad Muslim had never become a good Christian.

This image of Saladin, which appears to have been unique in Joinville's time, can be traced back to the Qur'an. Verse 256 of the second sura begins with the statement: "There is no compulsion in religion." Over the course of Islamic history, this Qur'anic injunction has had thoroughly practical implications. For example, during the end of the reign of the Fatimid caliph al-Hakim (d. 1021) and at the beginning of the reign of his successor, all those who had been compelled to convert to Islam during al-Hakim's persecutions were permitted to return to their old religions. During Saladin's reign, this principle was also taken to heart, as is made clear by the example of the famous Jewish scholar Maimonides when he left his homeland in Andalusia and traveled to Egypt. In Cairo, an Andalusian jurist complained that Maimonides had converted to Islam while living in Andalusia and therefore should be condemned for apostasy. Al-Qadi al-Fadil, Saladin's leading advisor, rejected the charge on the basis that a forced conversion to Islam is not valid. Experiences during the Third Crusade may have strengthened the views of Saladin and his entourage regarding this question. According to Western sources, Muslims who fell into Christian captivity accepted baptism because they feared for their lives, but they rejected Christianity as soon as they could. As a result, the kings of England and France, Richard Lionheart and Philip II Augustus, are reported to have issued a general prohibition against such baptisms.

Nevertheless, it would be wrong to see Saladin as a ruler who overstepped the boundaries of his Sunni Muslim upbringing and honored the Enlightenment ideal of tolerance. Admittedly, in contrast to many Muslim rulers he did permit those of different faiths who lived in his empire the degree of freedom that was permitted by Islam. However, in contrast to the image in Lessing's parable of the three rings, he likely held with the general Muslim view of Judaism and Christianity as two earlier forms of the one and only true religion, founded by Muhammad, that had superseded them. In any case, Saladin was deeply impressed by the Crusaders' complete commitment to their religion, which he stressed in his propaganda directed toward other Muslims.

The Champion of Freedom

Before the nineteenth century, Muslims had very little interest in the Crusades or in European affairs. Their interest in Saladin was hardly any greater, despite the fact that he had reconquered Jerusalem and, from the

Sunni perspective, had overthrown the heretical Fatimids. Some contemporary Muslims saw him as a second Joseph of Egypt or celebrated him as the Mahdi expected at the end of time. Not a few, however, saw him as a usurper of the inheritance of his predecessors Zengi and Nur al-Din and thought he had simply used the jihad against the Franks as a means of legitimizing his own power, and expanding it, at the expense of his Muslim neighbors.

The first modern biography of Saladin penned by an Easterner appeared in 1872 in Turkish. The writer was the Young Ottoman writer Namik Kemal. He intended, in part, to provide a Muslim answer to the seven-volume "Histoire des croisades," published by the Frenchman Joseph François Michaud during the years 1812–1822.

At the end of the nineteenth century, it was common among the leading politicians and intellectuals in the Ottoman empire to observe parallels between the policies of contemporary European powers and the Crusades. Thus, for example, Sultan Abdulhamid II, who ruled from 1876 to 1909, frequently expressed the view that Europe was engaged in a political crusade against his empire. These views were disseminated in the pan-Islamic press. One can also find references to these views in the introduction to the first comprehensive presentation of the Crusades by an Arab Muslim, which was published in Cairo in 1899. The author of this work was the Egyptian 'Ali al-Hariri.

The growing interest in the Crusades brought Saladin's image to the attention of many Muslims. They learned at the same time that this ruler had a positive image in Europe that stood in stark contrast to the negative view of most Europeans regarding other personalities in Islamic history. William II, the German emperor, held a positive view of Saladin. In 1898, he took a journey to the Near East organized by Thomas Cook during which he visited Saladin's tomb in Damascus. As a result of the speech that he gave there, millions of Muslims became aware of the esteem in which Saladin was held by Europeans. Among other remarks, William II said that he was "deeply moved by the thought that he was standing in the place where one of the most chivalrous rulers of all time, the great sultan Saladin, had spent time, a knight without fear or blemish, who often had to instruct his opponents in the art of chivalry." The emperor left a silk banner and a bronzed laurel wreath on Saladin's grave. Two decades later, these were taken as booty by Lawrence of Arabia and brought back to England, where they are still located, in the Imperial War Museum in London.

Arabic literature in the following decades did not lack for expressions of amazement regarding Saladin. Very early on, Christian Arab authors joined the mix, since it was a matter of current concern for them to honor a ruler who was tolerant of non-Muslims. By the last quarter of the nineteenth century, plays were being presented about Saladin by Egyptian and Lebanese theater groups, whose members frequently were Christians.

The first noteworthy biography of Saladin in modern Arabic literature was written by a Muslim author, the Egyptian Ahmad al-Biyali. It was first published in Cairo in 1920. After the end of the First World War and the collapse of the Ottoman empire, during the period of the British mandate over Palestine, references to Saladin were no longer separable from the political rhetoric of the Arab resistance to the plans of the Zionists. Following the Second World War and the subsequent foundation of the State of Israel, there was a veritable flood of literature in the Arabic-speaking world concerning the Crusades and their Muslim opponents, among whom Saladin was the most celebrated. Not least, the academic historiography drew numerous parallels between the establishment and destruction of the kingdom of Jerusalem on the one hand, and the history of the State of Israel on the other. This comparison often served the goal of awakening and maintaining over decades hopes for the destruction of Israel.

The memory of Saladin also plays an important role in the ongoing conflict between Arab and Kurdish nationalists. While modern Kurdish literature has seized upon Saladin as a hero of their nation, various governments in Baghdad, for example, have attempted to use Saladin as a symbol for pan-Islamic brotherhood and have fought in his name against Kurdish efforts to gain independence. Some Arab historians have tried to demonstrate that, at least culturally, Saladin was completely Arab, and that the great majority of his troops were also Arabs. In Turkey, by contrast, some authors claimed that the Kurds are descended from the Turks of Central Asia, and that Saladin is, therefore, a Turk.

Numerous Muslim heads of state, among whom most recently was Saddam Hussein, who also was born in Tikrit, have been all too happy to compare themselves with Saladin. However, in the eyes of many of today's Muslims, Saladin is by no means the champion of Islam and the unity of Muslims, as he attempted to portray himself in his propaganda. Indeed, in the view of Shi'ites, he is to be counted among the enemies of true Islam because he was the one who destroyed the Fatimid caliphate.

1138	The birth of Saladin in Tikrit
1144	The capture of Edessa by Zengi
1147–1148	The Second Crusade
1153	The capture of Ascalon by Baldwin III of Jerusalem
1154	The union of Aleppo and Damascus under the rule of Nur al-Din
1169	The conquest of Egypt by Nur al-Din's general Shirkuh; following Shirkuh's death, Saladin is named the vizier of the Fatimid caliphate
1171	The destruction of the Fatimid caliphate by Saladin and the return of Egypt to Islamic orthodoxy
1174	The death of Nur al-Din and Amalric of Jerusalem; Saladin takes power in Damascus
1175	Saladin's first victory over the combined forces of Aleppo and Mosul at the Horns of Hamah; recognition of Saladin by the 'Abbasid caliph as the ruler of Egypt and Syria, aside from Aleppo
1176	Saladin's second victory over Aleppo and Mosul at the battle of Tall al-Sultan; Saladin's marriage to Nur al-Din's widow 'Ismat al-Din Khatun
1177	Saladin's defeat at the hands of Baldwin IV of Jerusalem at Ramla
1179	Saladin's victory over Baldwin IV at the battle of Marj 'Uyun
1181	The accession to power at Aleppo by 'Izz al-Din of Mosul
1182	Saladin's failed attack on Mosul

1183	Frankish raid on the Red Sea; Saladin's capture of Aleppo; Saladin's attacks on the kingdom of Jerusalem
1185	Saladin's second attack on Mosul
1186	'Izz al-Din's recognition of Saladin's overlordship
1187	Saladin's victory over the Franks at the battle of Hattin; the conquest of Jerusalem and the greater part of the kingdom
1188	Saladin's conquests in the Crusader states of Tripoli and Antioch
1188–1192	The Third Crusade
1190	The death of Emperor Frederick Barbarossa in modern-day Turkey
1191	The capture of Acre by the crusaders; Saladin's defeat at the hands of Richard Lionheart at the battle of Arsuf
1192	Truce between Saladin and Richard Lionheart for three years and eight months
1193	Saladin's death in Damascus

Ehrenkreutz, Andrew S. *Saladin*. Albany, N.Y., 1972.

Elisséeff, Nikita. *Nūr ad-Dīn. Un grand prince musulman de Syrie au temps des croisades (511–569 H./1118–1174)*, 3rd edition. Damascus, 1967.

Ende, Werner. "Wer ist ein Glaubensheld, wer ist ein Ketzer? Konkurrierende Geschichtsbilder in der modernen Literatur islamischer Länder," in *Die Welt des Islams* N.S. 23–24 (1984): 70–94.

Gibb, Hamilton. *The Life of Saladin from the Works of ʿImād ad-Dīn and Bahāʾ ād-Dīn*. Oxford, 1973.

Hamilton, Bernard. *The Leper King and His Heirs: Baldwin IV and the Crusader Kingdom of Jerusalem*. Cambridge, 2000.

Hehl, Ernst-Dieter. "Was ist eigentlich ein Kreuzzug?" in *Historische Zeitschrift* 259 (1994): 297–336.

Herde, Peter. "Die Kämpfe bei den Hörnern von Hittīn und der Untergang des Kreuzritterheeres (3. und 4. Juli 1187)," in *Römische Quartalschrift für christliche Altertumskunde und Kirchengeschichte* 61 (1966): 1–50.

Hillenbrand, Carole. *The Crusades: Islamic Perspectives*. Edinburgh, 1999.

Holt, P. M. *The Age of the Crusades: The Near East from the Eleventh Century to 1517*. London/New York, 1986.

Humphreys, R. Stephen. *From Saladin to the Mongols: The Ayyubids of Damascus, 1193–1260*. Albany, N.Y., 1977.

Jubb, Margaret. *The Legend of Saladin in Western Literature and Historiography*. Lewiston, N.Y., 2000.

Kedar, Benjamin Z. *Crusade and Mission: European Approaches toward the Muslims*. Princeton, N.J., 1984.

——. (ed.). *The Horns of Hattīn*. Jerusalem/London, 1992.

Köhler, Michael A. *Allianzen und Verträge zwischen fränkischen und islamischen Herrschern im Vorderen Orient. Eine Studie über das zwischenstaatliche Zusammenleben vom 12. bis ins 13. Jahrhundert*. Berlin/New York, 1991.

Labib, Subhi Y. *Handelsgeschichte Ägyptens im Spätmittelalter (1171–1517).* Wiesbaden, 1965.

Lane-Poole, Stanley. *Saladin and the Fall of the Kingdom of Jerusalem.* London/New York, 1898.

Lev, Yaacov. *Saladin in Egypt.* Leiden/Boston/Cologne, 1999.

——. "The Social and Economic Policies of Nūr al-Dīn (1146–1174): The Sultan of Syria," in *Der Islam* 81 (2004): 218–242.

Lyons, Malcolm Cameron, and D. E. P. Jackson. *Saladin: The Politics of the Holy War.* Cambridge, 1982.

Mayer, Hans Eberhard. *Die Kreuzfahrerherrschaft Montréal (Sōbak): Jordanien im 12. Jahrhundert.* Wiesbaden, 1990.

Möhring, Hannes. *Saladin und der Dritte Kreuzzug: Aiyubidische Strategie und Diplomatie im Vergleich vornehmlich der arabischen mit den lateinischen Quellen.* Wiesbaden, 1980.

——. "Heiliger Krieg und politische Pragmatik: Salahadinus Tyrannus," in *Deutsches Archiv* 39 (1983): 417–466.

——. "Kreuzzug und Dschihad in der mediaevistischen und orientalischen Forschung 1965–1985," in *Innsbrucker Historische Studien* 10/11 (1988): 361–386.

——. "Der andere Islam: Zum Bild vom toleranten Sultan Saladin und neuen Propheten Schah Ismail," in *Die Begegnung des Westens mit dem Osten,* ed. von O. Engels and P. Schreiner. Sigmaringen, 1993, pp. 131–155.

——. "Mekkawallfahrten orientalischer und afrikanischer Herrscher im Mittelalter," in *Oriens* 34 (1994): 314–329.

——. "Zwischen Joseph-Legende und Mahdī-Erwartung: Erfolge und Ziele Sultan Saladins im Spiegel zeitgenössischer Dichtung und Weissagung," in *War and Society in the Eastern Mediterranean, 7th–15th Centuries,* ed. von Y. Lev. Leiden/New York/Cologne, 1997, pp. 177–223.

——. "Die Kreuzfahrer, ihre muslimischen Untertanen und die heiligen Stätten des Islam," in *Toleranz im Mittelalter,* ed. von A. Patschovsky and H. Zimmermann, Sigmaringen, 1998, pp. 129–157.

——. "Zwei aiyūbidische Briefe an Alexander III. und Lucius III. bei Radulf de Diceto zum Kriegsgefangenenproblem," in *Archiv für Diplomatik* 46 (2000): 197–216.

——. *König der Könige: Der Bamberger Reiter in neuer Interpretation.* Königstein, 2004.

Noth, Albrecht. *Heiliger Krieg und Heiliger Kampf in Islam und Christentum: Beiträge zur Vorgeschichte und Geschichte der Kreuzzüge.* Bonn, 1966.

Rabie, Hassanein. *The Financial System of Egypt A.H. 564–741/A.D. 1169–1341.* London, 1972.

Richards, D. S. "The Early History of Saladin," in *Islamic Quarterly* 17 (1973): 140–159.

Riley-Smith, Jonathan (ed.). *Großer Bildatlas der Kreuzzüge*. Freiburg/Basel/Vienna, 1992.

——— (ed.). *Illustrierte Geschichte der Kreuzzüge*. Frankfurt/New York, 1999.

Sauvaget, Jean. "Le Cénotaphe de Saladin," in *Revue des arts asiatiques* 6 (1929–1930): 168–175.

Setton, Kenneth M. (ed.). *A History of the Crusades*, 6 vols. Philadelphia/Madison, 1955–1989.

Sivan, Emmanuel. *L'Islam et la Croisade: Idéologie et propagande dans les réactions Musulmanes aux Croisades*. Paris, 1968.

———. "Modern Arab Historiography of the Crusades," in *Asian and African Studies* 8 (1972): 109–149.

———. "Saladin et le calife al-Māsir," in *Scripta Hierosolymitana*, vol. 23, *Studies in History*. Jerusalem, 1972, pp. 126–145.

———. Mythes politiques arabes. Paris, 1995.

Smail, R. C. *Crusading Warfare (1097–1193)*. Cambridge, 1956.